From Whence to Where

UNDERSTANDING MEMORY-EMOTION-CONCEPTS

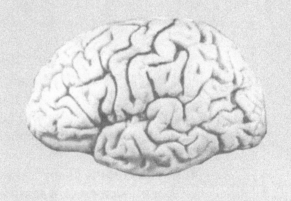

THE CREATION OF LEARNING, KNOWLEDGE AND
PROGRAMING IN THE BRAIN

By

Dr. Bruce Brown

TURNER PUBLISHING COMPANY

Copyright © 1997
Publishing Rights: Turner Publishing Company

Turner Publishing Company Staff:
Editor: Herbert C. Banks II
Designer: Holly Coleman

Library of Congress Catalog Card No. 97-60396
ISBN: 978-1-68162-336-8

Limited Edition. Additional copies may be
purchased directly from the publisher.

TABLE OF CONTENTS

PREFACE

It has taken 20 years to write this book. It is a book about thinking, deciding, acting and creating. It explains how we learn, store knowledge, and revise our knowledge throughout life.

It is a new theory of brain and cell functions. This page is for reference to the technical terms.

Neuropeptides are "molecules of short chains of amino acids (such as endorphins, enkephalines and vasopressins) found in brain and nerve tissue synapses." They include enzymes, endocrines, hormones, antibodies, anti-rejection drugs, narcotics, antibiotics, atomic radiation, or any molecular configurations that perform like emotions.

Neuropeptide emotions provide the impetus for brain and body cell functions and are defined as "physiological departures from homeostasis that are subjectively experienced in strong feelings (love, hate, desire, fear, hunger, thirst, fatigue, etc.) and manifest themselves in neuromuscular, respiratory, cardiovascular, hormonal and other bodily changes preparatory to overt acts, which may or may not be performed."

These emotions are stored as Memory-Emotion-Concepts, called MECs for short.

MECs have unique properties: They can be recalled, modified and restored as long as one lives. This is the heart of the new theory of brain and cell functions.

"No matter what reason tells us,
　　　　It is only when our emotions are,
　　　　　　　Appealed to and enlisted, that
　　　　　　　　　We truly speak from the heart."
　　　　　　　　　Max Brandt

"Memories are the father of thoughts;
　　　　Thoughts conjure decisions;
　　　　　　　Decisions lead to actions;
　　　　　　　　　Thoughts, decisions and actions;
　　　　　　　　　　　Produce our creations, the MECs;
　　　　　　　　　　　　　Which are unique for each of us."
　　　　　　　　　　　　　　Dr. Bruce Brown

MECS THEORY

"Emotions are a physiological departure from homeostasis that is subjectively experienced in strong (?) feelings (love, hate, desire, fear, hunger, thirst, fatigue, etc.) and manifest themselves in neuromuscular, respiratory, cardiovascular, hormonal and other bodily changes preparatory to overt acts which may or may not be performed."

1. Homeostasis evolved to insure survival and reproduction; while memory-emotion-concepts (MECS) evolved as the method for maintaining metabolic equilibrium.

2. Memory-Emotion-Concepts (MECS) in cell receptors are the means of learning. They catalyze incoming neuropeptide stimuli into NEW MECS responses. These NEW MECS are the stored memories and knowledge in the cells and reflect the responses to stimuli from hereditary and acquired experiences from the beginning of life.

3. Recall of MECS initiate the biofeedback chain reactions and parallel processings through centers, called maps, that lead to more learning and improved responses to stimuli. Dr. Allman at Caltech describes processing centers or "maps" that coordinate multiple systems of visual function. One cell dealing with motion, another with shape and another with color, etc. He has also found evidence of myriad maps that parallel process intracellular interactions throughout the body. Example:

4. The antelope must see, recognize and remember the danger of the charging lion. The decision is instant flight, entailing coordinated muscle actions, faster heart and breathing rates; choosing an escape route; attaining maximum speed and performing evasive maneuvers.

5. The new (MECS), which are new molecules with electromotive force (EMFS) and polarities (PS), are added memories stored as engrams of knowledge.

6. Neuropeptide stimuli, being catalyzed by the receptor (MECS) into responses, is similar to a key unlocking the door. Stimuli have specific molecular configurations which fit those of the receptor (MECS).

7. MECS may be subject to "extinction," "intensification" and "modification" over periods of time.

The chain reactions and parallel processings of Memory-Emotion-Concepts (MECS) are the first step of thinking in the brain and are called Propagation and/or the Process of Recall.

Discrimination is the second step of thinking, requiring evaluation of those (MECS) that excite (+) and/or inhibit (-) homeostasis. Processing the Mecs.

Summation is the third step of thinking by which all the electromotive forces (EMFS) and polarities (PS) of the MECS, are added, to form thoughts, decisions, actions and creations.

The recall of the (MECS) may be conscious, subconscious, but never voluntary.

Thinking will continue until the Electromotive Forces (EMFS) and Polarities (PS) become too weak to father decisions. Thoughts, decisions, actions and creations are the involuntary summation of MECS stimuli and responses. The definition of Thought; "the power to conceive or realize."

They are original creations for people, animals, plants, birds or micro-organism cells, This is applicable to all five kingdoms of all family trees.

The involuntary and original summation of stimuli-catalysis-responses, called MECS will create thoughts, decisions and actions, completing the cycle of a cellular and/or brain function.

Thinking processess will continue until the EMFS and PS are exhausted.

It is hoped that these concepts will nullify the cherished myths that man controls his own destiny. Perhaps they will make artificial intelligence accessible and make rehabilitation of the hemiplegic feasible. Criminal acts will be recognized as the results of a lifetime of anti-social conditioning.

Criminals might be stimulated by neuropeptides that will catalyze MECS compatible with society or, if intractable, swift capital punishment be meted out for the common good, relieving the ever mounting over-crowding and costly maintenance of the jails. Alcoholism, smoking, drug addiction, obesity and many habits are examples of emotions out of control.

Divorce and angers are classic emotional forces precipitating foolish decisions.

Wars, strikes and riots occur and succeed when we listen to or read inflammatory opinions by outside stimuli. Salesmen and advertising of all kinds feed on man's emotional vanities, egos, desires, lusts and greed. Married couples and their children learn early what emotional strings to pull to gain their objectives. The family pet knows the master's weaknesses.

It is possible to demonstrate that the stimuli we receive throughout our lives will create the MECS in our cells. This is the learning process.

THEORY OF BRAIN FUNCTIONS:

THINKING, FEELING (EMOTIONS), THEN ACTING

Dedicated to the memory of Dr. Wilder Penfield, renowned neurosurgeon; to my friend D.H. Ralston; to Professor Max Snider of Lehigh University and, especially, to my sympathetic wife, Denise, who listened to my orating, patiently waded through my writing, and still came up with many helpful suggestions.

9/26/96

Brain and Cell Function, a new theory (1965), pinpoints the how, when and where of patient's thinking, as a means of restoring normal function to the hemiplegic.

In 1965 I became interested in the "living Hell" of the hemiplegic, a prisoner within his own body.

How do cells receive and store information; how is it recalled; how modified; how restored? This pursuit led to a new theory of brain and cell functions.

It evolves as follows;

a. When neuropeptide motor stimuli are received by the cell receptors, a part of each and every cell, they are catalyzed into sensory responses. These responses are Memory-Emotion-Concepts or MECs. They create the learning, knowledge and programming in each cell. MECs can be recalled, modified and then restored as New-MECs through chain reaction biofeedbacks and parallel processing by the neural networks.

b. There is, as well, a communication between every cell of the body with every other cell through the neural, vascular and lymphatic channels of the Psychoneuroimmunolgy Systems.

The ambivalence of MECs is clearly expressed by the Definition of Neuropeptides; "Any of the molecules of short chains of amino acids (endorphins, enkephalins vasopressin, etc.) found in brain tissue and body cells, classified as putative neuro-transmitters, although some are hormones." An expanded concept would include enzymes, endocrines, hormones, anti-bodies, cytokines, interferons, DNA-RNA, thalidomides, antitissue-rejection drugs, narcotics, antibiotics, atomic radiation, or any molecular configurations that perform like emotions. Neuropeptides are emotions.

Emotions Defined: "Emotions are a physiological departure from homeostasis that is subjectively experienced in strong feelings such as (love, hate, desire, fear, hunger, thirst, fatigue, etc.) and manifest themselves in neuromuscular, respiratory, cardiovascular, hormonal and other bodily changes preparatory to overt acts which may or may not be performed."

Emotions have more facets than there are words in *Webster's Unabridged Dictionary*.

THERE ARE THREE STEPS OF LEARNING:

1. PROPAGATION, is the first step of learning. When MECs are recalled they initiate chain reaction biofeedbacks and parallel processings through neural networks and through the vascular and lymphatic channels of the Psychoneuroimmunology Systems interconnect all cells of the body.

2. DISCRIMINATION; is the second step. There are responses to stimuli which are (exciting, and/or inhibiting) for cell homeostasis and physiologic equilibrium.

3. SUMMATION is the third step of learning. This step calculates the electromotive forces (EMFs) and polarities (PS) or propagation and discrimination in cells and initiates (thoughts?), decisions, actions and creations. Summations are determined by stimuli intensities, durations, timings and repetitions.

MECs ARE MOLECULAR AGGREGATES

Responses to stimuli are comparable to the dialing of a telephone number, wherein the calling stimuli are Catalyzed by the switchboard's Relays to the telephone number being called.

Reference; "How Neural Networks Learn from Experience" Geoffrey E. Hinton, *Scientific American*, September 1992.

Dr. Hinton describes hidden weight input data as the stimuli, with biofeedback chain reactions and parallel processings summating the output. This is comparable to the propagation, discrimination and summation of the MECs.

MAGNETIC DISCS AS "ROSETTA STONES"

Memory-Emotion-Concepts (MECs) as magnetic discs. How emotions are the keys to brain functions of; Thought, Decisions, Actions and Creations. All discs have equal EMFs and PS for simplicity.

SUMMATING ELECTRICAL CHARGES TO MAKE DECISIONS

MECs; Reasons to buy a car   SCORES
1. Sufficient money in the bank.
2. Need a car to get to work.
3. Old car too costly to repair.   (+3)

MECs: Reasons against buying
1. Insufficient money in the bank.
2. Public transport available.
3. Loan interest rates too high.   (-3)

MECs: Wait 6 months to buy
1. Savings account will be up.
2. Expect a Xmas Bonus.   (+2)
3. Train takes one hour longer.
4. If car fails, no vacation.   (-2)   (0)

MECs: Buy in 3 months.
1. Savings account will be up.
2. Expect a Xmas bonus.   (+2)
3. Train takes one hour longer.
4. If car fails, no vacation.   (-2)   (0)
5. Inheritance from aunt in 3 months.   Total   (+1)

Thoughts, decisions, actions and creations will propagate, discriminate and summate MECs by similar processes.

MECs are hereditary and instinctual from the beginning of life or acquired and environmental from the moment of conception. They are continuously modified throughout life, dependent on the stimuli they receive and/or perceive, and their intensity, repetition, duration and timing.

DISCUSSION OF INTRACELLUAR FUNCTIONS

11/12/96

When recall neuropeptides are catalyzed by cell receptor MECs, the responses initiate Propagations. This is a process of chain reaction biofeedbacks, and parallel processings through the neural networks, and through the vascular and lymphatic channels of the psychoneuroimmunology systems that link every cell of the body with every other cell. This recalls the information and programming contained in the MECs. This may be conscious but the majority is subconscious or subliminal.

Decision arise from the foundations of our hereditary instincts of survival and reproduction but are molded and shaped by the environmental influences and pressures we sustain from the moment of fertilization to the end of life.

The significance of any MECs will be proportional to the percentages and intensities of their components of punishment and reward. MECs are non-volitional emotions and, contrary to common belief, are not governed by reason and logic.

The principles are the same as we ascend the evolutionary ladder, but in place of the one-cell paramecium, we now have 100 billion neurons, 100 trillion connections and trillions (?) of body cells, communicating and feeding back to the brain.

The key theme is that Memories, alias Engrams of Education, alias Emotion Concepts (MECs), alias Conditioning; are essential to receive and perceive the stimuli to which the brain and body are subjected. Stimuli may originate from two sources:

A. Internal; The permanent programmed memories in the DNA, which control the autonomic functions of physiology, catalyzing the stimuli from physiologic changes in the body into motor responses which then act as stimuli to return the body to a state of equilibrium.

B. External; The continuously-modified programmed memories in the body cells catalyze sensory stimuli into motor responses by chain reaction biofeedbacks and parallel processings. They are stored as New MECs and increase the sum of one's learning. The stimuli from A and B summate, propagate and discriminate thoughts, decisions, actions and creations.

HYPOTHESIS

The programmed instructions of the DNA and the RNA are MECs, catalyzing the neuropeptide motor stimuli they received and perceive into sensory responses. These responses create the succession of neuropeptides that trigger the growth processes of the fertilized ovum, initiating the schedules for the maturation of the newborn, similar to the programmed growth for all living organisms.

These same instructions may some day rehabilitate the capricious destruction of brain organization in the hemiplegic, which leaves myriad areas of normal but inaccessible hardware in the brain.

Brain and body cell functions, reduced to a one-cell operation, postulate that all body cells function as receptors. When "neuropeptide?" stimuli are catalyzed by the receptors in the cells the responses create MECs, which are engrams of knowledge, fathering our thoughts, ideas, decisions, actions and creations.

MECs are molecular structures with electromotive forces (EMFs) and polarities (PS) with exciting (EX+) or inhibiting (IN-) effects on the maintenance of metabolic equilibrium of the organism, requirements for survival and reproduction.

The chapter on DNA and RNA contains more aspects of DNA-RNA functions.

The catalysis of stimuli into MECs responses is similar to the familiar telephone switchboard. The numbers being dialed are the stimuli; the switchboard relays catalyse the stimuli into responses that ring the telephone number being called. Switchboard relays have fixed response patterns that must be reprogrammed by the telephone engineers, while MECs responses are reprogrammed with each stimulus received.

Memory is the father of thought and thought is the father of decisions.

In tracing the origin of emotions concepts MECs, it is postulated that emotions evolved with the beginning of life to insure survival and reproduction of the species. In the primordial soup, organisms had hunger, recognized danger (fear), faced threatening environments (fight or flight), and the need to have parthenogenesis or bisexual reproduction (sex). These emotions are but a few of many needed to catalyze the response requirements for existence. Such emotions are the memories and education (engrams), evolved over eons of time, which account for our thoughts, decisions, actions and creations of today.

11/10/96

Brain function may be cognitive, conscious or subconscious and involuntary. Body cell functions are subconscious and involuntary.

Brain and body cell functions are nothing more than stimuli, external or internal, being catalyzed by receptors into responses. Receptors are MECs or catalysts, transforming stimuli into responses.

We are born, live and die as summations of all the Memory-Emotion-Concepts (MECs) within ourselves. We neither have Will-power or Won't Power.

Having inherited Ego as a necessary requirement for survival, we resent the implication that we are not masters of our own ship. Only a moment of contemplation, if we are honest, and we should concede that we are the slaves of our emotions. Pull the string and the monkey climbs, descending when the string is relaxed.

When a MECs is stimulated, the response will depend on the molecular structure of the neuropeptide that keys into it. Allergic reactions to antigens are familiar catalytic phenomena; the sudden withdrawal of the hand touching a hot stove is a catalytic response to the emotion pain. The MECs of immunity and pain are catalysts leading to the responses but not a part of them, awaiting the next stimuli.

10-29-96

When the neuropeptides of Recall are catalyzed by the MECs, the responses initiate Propagations. This is the process of chain reaction biofeedbacks and parallel processings through the neural networks and through vascular and lymphatic channels of the psychoneuroimmune systems by which every body cell communicates with every other body cell.

As an example; a painful blister on the heel informs the brain and the brain relays the message to conscious awareness and to the muscles, joints and nerves leading to limping or removal of the shoe. At the same time, the recalled MECs illuminate and display all the facets and memories of blisters. In the process, more facets of knowledge of heel blisters are added to and restored as a New MECs. This is the first step of learning. Gas pains sending us to the bathroom are another example.

Learning from Experience: Biofeedback chain reactions and parallel processings are the means of creating MECs. The enormity of the processes are staggering. There are 50,000,000,000 neurons all interconnected through the axons and dendrites. Learning to walk or to throw a baseball requires 1,000's of repetitions. Each act of repetition is modified by the recall of the learned knowledge (Old MECs) resulting from the prior trials and errors.

Each repetition adds more knowledge, (New MECs) and increased proficiency in walking and throwing.

Conscious defined; knowing or perceiving something within oneself or a fact about oneself.

Propagation results when Old knowledge is recalled.

Discrimination is choosing New knowledge that is exciting or inhibiting for the survival and reproduction of the organism or cell.

Summation consolidates propagation and discrimination into the responses of decisions, actions and creations; adding New Learning to knowledge or adding to the data bank.

"Accelerated Rehabilitation of the Hemiplegic" is based on identical learning processes. The hemiplegic must re-entrain his lifetime of propagation, discrimination and summation through new channels to access the islands of normal knowledge surviving the stroke. There is evidence that some neurons can sprout plumes of dendrites.

We have described emotion concepts as simple entities. In reality they are a very complex mixture of molecular hereditary and acquired EMFs and PS.

It is easier to understand, if we can relate to something familiar. A symphony orchestra recital might be likened to the function of a neuron. The music composition would be the stimuli; the conductor the emotion concept; who interprets (catalyzes) the stimuli into instructions to the musicians; who produce the response harmonies; the resulting music becomes the sensory stimuli to the audience. It will be interpreted according to the individual's musical appreciation and his personal concepts. The interpretations will determine the pleasures they receive. Comparing, again, to a neuron, the response from the original neuron (the musical score) is now transmitted to a host of other neurons (the audience) and they in turn to more neurons, (like children and friends). These would be the chain reactions of brain function.

THE CREATION OF EMOTION CONCEPTS IN THE FIRST YEAR

The newborn starts with no concepts, other than his hereditary reflexes and metabolic functions, etc. We are going to use "Orange" as an emotion concept. In addition, creation of a concept will depend upon the summation of the EMFs and PS of the stimuli, which the newborn will receive or perceive through his senses of sight, sound, smell, taste, touch. The responses will be proportional to the intensity, duration, timing and repetition of the stimuli. All Memory-Emotion-Concepts or MECs have a "How, When and Where."

To illustrate the formulation of an emotion concept, we have arbitrarily chosen some overly-simplified initial concepts of the newborn infant as a foundation for the proliferation and discrimination of stimuli, leading to the modified and complex concepts that comprise Education.

The newborn follows the ball swinging on a string over the crib —Visual and Pattern Recognition stimuli. He hears the word "Ball" from his admirers —sound stimuli. Then mama says "Orange Juice" as she feeds him —sound and taste.

He sees the orange-red sunset (sight and round pattern.) He crawls over daddy's shoes of pebble-grain leather—touch and rough stimuli. Someone gives him an orange to play with and uses the word "Orange" —color and firm to touch.

At this point, his summation of "Orange" will be:
   a. Spherical like a ball, that rolls on the floor.
   b. Sweet to taste.
   c. Orange like the sunset.
   d. Rough like daddy's shoes.
   e. Firm like the floor.

To explain how sensory stimuli lead to entrainment of engrams in a process of proliferation and discrimination, we will consider the concepts of ball, sweet, orange, rough and firm as simple and single entities.

Evolution of the Concept "Orange"

The subject will be an infant under one year of age, who already has the capacity to grasp, focus eyes, crawl, taste, hear and smell.

1. An orange is placed in the infant's hand. The stimulus is identical to an earlier contact with a ball, which we will call the Emotion Concept "Ball". At this point, he interprets Orange as round like a ball, that Rolls.

2. The infant watches his mother squeeze the juice of an orange into a glass and give it to him to drink. Now he interprets Orange as round like a ball and sweet to taste.

3. The infant had seen the orange color of a sunset while sitting on his mother's lap. When he sees an Orange, now, he interprets "round like a ball, sweet to taste, the color orange of the sunset."

4. When the infant crawled over daddy's shoes of pebble grain leather he felt the roughness. When grasping the orange he experienced the same tactile sensation. Now the interpretation of orange is "round like a ball, sweet to taste, orange color like the sunset and rough like daddy's shoes, that rolls."

5. As the infant crawls he finds the floor to be firm, similar to the firm texture of an orange. Now he interprets an orange to be "round like a ball, sweet to taste, orange color like the sunset, rough like daddy's shoes and firm to touch."

All of the sensory stimuli described above have evolved by proliferation into the Orange Concept. Each of the five stimuli is capable of recalling this concept, now in memory. By the process of discrimination the Orange Concept is now "round, sweet, color orange, rough skinned and firm, that rolls." This is comparable to the If-Then of Basic Computer Programming.

Stimulation of our memories, engrams, emotion concepts, all synonyms, induces thinking. Thinking provokes thought. Thought leads to decisions, decisions to actions and actions to creations.

This now follows the paths of learning, which are Proliferation and Propagation first step; then Discrimination between pleasing or disturbing stimuli; and finally the Summation and storing of this Knowledge in the brain cells, where it can be recalled, modified and restored.

This unique learning method has been evolving over millions of years and produces birthing or creation, living and learning and, finally, aging and death.

The 1-year-old is only acting out the master plan laid down by his creator.

The proliferation and discrimination of the "Orange" concept is identical in principle in all living creatures of the five kingdoms of animals, plants, fungi, protists and monera.

The 1-year-old acquires better muscular coordination, emerging vocal vocabulary and articulation, refined recognition of people and objects, discrimination and cataloging of sound, sight, taste, smell and touch.

Step by step the concepts are proliferated and fine-tuned (discrimination). This expanding concept of orange will depend on the intensity, duration, timing and repetition of each stimuli. Reception of stimuli is not the same as its perception in many cases. The exciting or inhibiting effects of the stimuli will create unique concepts for that individual.

CONCEPT CREATION FROM 6 YEARS TO DEATH

Following the cradle to pre-school era are more and more schooling and increasingly complex relationships with people and activities in the environment, creating and increasing the bank of MECs.

MECs ARE UNIQUE FOR EACH PERSON

No one knows the limits of the concepts that a brain can store in its bank.

With the immensity and complication of the MECs, we forget that they are nothing more than arrangements of protons and electrons within the atoms that comprise the molecules of memory with varying EMFs (Electromotive Forces) and PS (Polarities). Whether they are received or perceived as "exciting" or "inhibiting" doesn't simplify our understanding.

The humbling thing is that the millions of year old paramecium have identical methods for learning.

Emotions are neuropeptides; they are physical entities, performing as stimuli or responses as conditions demand. They are the foundation stones of all learning.

Emotions: "They are not cognitive and volitional states of consciousness."

Peptides (neuropeptides) are defined: various amides that are derived from two or more amino acids by combination of the amino group of one acid with the carboxyl group of another and are usually obtained by partial hydrolysis of proteins. Emotion-neuropeptides are the stimuli that trigger catalysis of the MECs in the cells.

Learning begins with stimuli from external or internal origin being received or perceived by cell receptors (MECs) and being catalyzed into responses.

These responses are the units of learning or engrams of knowledge and are New MECs.

Stimuli intensity, timing, duration and repetition determine the cell receptor responses. Learning responses will be accepted or rejected by the organism, dependent on the degree they excite or inhibit homeostasis, thereby, enhancing or diminishing the chances of survival and reproduction.

When emotion-neuropeptide stimuli lock into specific cell receptors they are catalyzed into responses, which initiate the chain reactions and parallel processings to other receptors. The Psychoneuroimmunology System through the neural, vascular and lymphatic channels is another pathway for stimuli to reach every cell of the body.

These other receptors are the MECs of prior learning, being derived from hereditary or instinctual learning or from acquired or environmental learning since conception.

Chain reactions and parallel processings account for thinking, thoughts, decisions, actions and creations. This is the way distant memories are catalyzed over and over until their intensity intrudes into our consciousness and cognition. The vast majority of chain reactions and parallel processings are subliminal.

Excessive intensity of chain reactions and parallel processings can overwhelm cognition and consciousness, leading to severe depressions, psychoses, shock, manic exhilaration, hysteria and any exaggerated responses to emotion-neuropeptide stimulation.

Memory-Emotion-Concepts And Cognitive, Conscious, Subconscious And Involuntary

9/30/96

Cognition is the act or process of knowing in the broadest sense. Storage of knowledge is the beginning of memories.

Consciousness is "awareness of sensations, perceptions, ideas, attitudes and feelings." These are Emotions.

"Knowing or perceiving something within oneself or a fact about oneself and affecting, thought, feeling and behavior without entering awareness" are our subconscious Concepts.

Memory-Emotion-Concepts create the MECs which are the total of all our learning, whether hereditary or acquired since conception. They are involuntary.

MECs programs are what drove the one-celled paramecium, for thousands of years.

They can retreat when colliding with an object, turn 45 degrees and then proceed forward, or retreat from a noxious environment, or seek palatable foods. Their responses are decisions leading to actions, evolved thousands of years before. This may be humbling to man's vanity to realize that mankind is not the first to make decisions, take actions, create responses, and reproduce. All living organisms, animals, plants and micro-organisms, have evolved their specific MECs to fit their own living patterns.

When MECs are recalled by key neuropeptide stimuli the responses initiate chain reaction biofeedbacks and parallel processing through the neural networks. The responses are the propagation, discrimination and summation of the MECs necessary for memory, learning and recall.

Birth, life and death are a summation of all the MECs within, be it a human, paramecium or others.

MECs And Emotion Concepts

9/29/96

In this paper, emotions will be dealt with as single entities for simplification. In reality, they are complex coded engrams of molecular configurations. They are a composite of exciting (EX) and inhibiting (IN) EMFs and PS blended by hereditary and environmentally acquired conditioning stimuli. To make matters more difficult, they are in a fluid state of reprogramming throughout life.

Chronologically they differ by age grouping:

1. Under three years of age, formulation of the emotions is primarily a process of receiving and perceiving stimulation from the environment (externally) and heredity (internally) with minimal motor responses. Memories are formulated as MECs, then, are summated into thoughts, to decisions, to actions and to creations;

This is a minimal function in this age group. Memories are the engrams of education and knowledge. However, MECs programming, in this age group, can only take place by the interaction, at the time of biologic maturation, of the hereditary MECs with Environmentally acquired MECs stimuli.

2. Three to 12 years is the beginning of feedback motor responses. Stimuli from the environment and heredity are now being catalyzed by the MECs into motor responses of thoughts, decisions, actions and creations. Immature and inappropriate motor responses are the hallmark of this phase.

3. Twelve to 20 years is the "What's For Me" period. Self-expression (physically, mentally and emotionally) challenging the world of survival and, even, reproduction.

4. Twenty to 45 years adds the dimension of "What's For You." MECs have now been tempered with experiences along life's paths. For Every Gain There Is A Price Tag. If we need help from others (need the security of the herd and benefits of colonization); need a mate to fulfill our biological urge; need answers to the unknowns beyond our control (religion among them); then we must give, share, love, cooperate and have faith. The gain is peace, joy, happiness and contentment.

5. After 45 years, the MECs we have forged in life are stabilized and the drives to survive and reproduce are diminishing and we can enjoy the "fruits of our labors."

EVOLUTION OF EMOTION CONCEPTS THROUGHOUT LIFE

Life is a continuing process for propagation, discrimination and summation of our MECs. For example:

Pain, such as the sting of a hornet, is an hereditary emotion concept permitting one to receive sensory stimuli, catalyze them into motor responses of escaping the stimuli or protesting the insult. Sensory stimuli received will be perceived differently by each person according to his individual and unique MECs. Each experience of pain propagates the emotion concepts to include the source, location and circumstances of that stimuli; to discriminate between the "exciting" or "inhibiting" components of the stimuli; and to summate the EMFs and PS of the stimuli into memory.

Now the new Pain MECs, subtitled "hornet", is an engram of education in memory, ready to catalyze the next hornet-stimuli into the motor responses of thought, decision, action and creation, based on the Newest MECs of pain-hornet at that moment.

Future MECs of pain may lead to an escape or protest of the stimuli by "just the buzz of a nearby hornet." As one can see, the emotion of Pain becomes a many-faceted concept in memory, involving many cells, many pathways and different areas of the brain.

Summation may lead to immediate motor responses, delayed responses or subtle responses that may or may not lead to overt acts.

Electromotive Forces (EMFs) And The Emotions

The intensity of the EMFs of MECs varies from person to person. These EMFs fluctuate throughout life, up or down, in proportion to the sensory stimuli received and their Exciting (EX) or Inhibiting (IN) components.

The Pain of a difficult labor or that of abdominal surgery has driven many a patient to state, "Never Again." The intensity of the paid is excruciating, the EMFs are high and the inhibiting component is strong.

Everyone knows another baby arrives and more surgery is performed; and everyone lashes out in anger, saying and doing things he regrets. These examples illustrate that sustained intense sensory stimuli are necessary for consistent motor responses.

Profiling Emotion Concepts (MECs)

As sensory stimuli are formulating our MECs into out memories of education which will catalyze our motor responses, it is apparent that is not the simple process alluded to earlier, but very complex.

Each stimuli received or perceived throughout our lives will have a How, When, Where and What. These stimuli may have been conscious, subconscious or forgotten, but, nevertheless, contributors to the MECs of the moment.

Since this is a quagmire of recall of the stimuli intensities, durations, timing and repetition, the only practical means of evaluating any MECs of any person is to provoke their responses to sight (words [read or spoken], pictures, objects and movies), touch (objects, skin contacts, pressures, temperatures), sounds (words, spoken or heard, music, or terrifying unknown noises), smells, tastes, position sensings (posturing) and, recently, feedbacks between the brain and the immune system of the PNI (psychoneuroimmunology).

Actually, there is a two-way feedback between all body cells and the central nervous system. Blisters on the heel make us limp; gas pains send us to the bathroom; noxious fumes make us cough; or a slap in the face makes us retaliate or move away.

REENTRAINMENT OF THE HEMIPLEGIC

Cerebral hemorrhages destroy only portions of one hemisphere, leaving a major portion of the brain intact on the affected side and normal in the other hemisphere. However, the feedback within the brain itself and that to the body has been disrupted by the stroke. Pathways, brain nuclei and some of the cortex have been destroyed. The MECs in these areas can no longer receive and perceive the sensory stimuli and catalyze the motor responses. The channels of transmission took a lifetime to propagate, discriminate and summate these MECs.

If the telephone switchboard is destroyed, the system is functionless. The switchboard function is similar to that of the MECs, e.g. catalyzing the caller telephone number into the receiver phone number. To reestablish function, new circuits in the switchboard and new feedback MECs between brain and body cells are required.

To reformulate MECs in the hemiplegic, it seems logical to use the most powerful concepts that insure survival and reproduction. We suggest fear, pain, sex and love.

Simultaneously, we suggest the most desired functions to be coordinated muscular movements, speech and summations of memories into thoughts, decisions, actions and creations.

A. Implantation or surface application of electrodes in those muscles needed to raise and lower the arm, flex and extend elbow, wrist and fingers with an electric stimulator available.

B. Immobilize the other arm and legs, in a comfortable sitting posture, thus eliminating feedback and motor responses by pre-hemiplegic channels.

C. Motion picture viewing of the movement to be reentrained, captioned with printed instructions of the goals.

D. Soothing background of music favored by patient.

E. The closest and most loving relative or friend present. Loving and sharing are sorely needed by hemiplegics.

F. Therapist or technician to give verbal instructions and commands, such as; "Raise or lower your arm"; "Bend or extend the elbow"; "Move the wrist"; "Flex and extend the fingers." If no response after a pause, then stimulation of the electrodes. Stimuli intensities, durations, timing and repetition to be determined by trial and error. A buzzer ringing just prior to the stimulation will be a warning. If the patient is able to carry out the command voluntarily, the movement will operate a switch to cancel the stimulation.

G. Liberal praise and encouragement for success and minimal scolding for failure.

H. Words spoken by the technician or family, simultaneous with the printed word on the screen and picture displayed if possible. Perhaps a charade acted out by the family or in a brief action movie.

I. Then command to "try and say the Word" with any guttural sound being accepted as success. No attempt to utter a sound to be followed by a pause, then the buzzer and electrical prod.

J. Family to write short scripts of memorable, pleasant or humorous incidents in the patient's past. This script to be printed no the screen and read out loud by the family, Slowly. Always Assume the Patient Understands Most or All of What is Being Seen or Heard. If Tears or Agitation Occur, Stop and Try Again Another Day or Rewrite the Script.

K. Try and establish a code of communication such as: Blinking the eyes once is "Yes" and twice is "No."

L. Pose questions for the patient to answer based on the incidents in the scripts, such as; "Do you remember how Billy laughed?" etc.

M. We know the patient has compartments of memory remaining all through the brain, although access by normal channels has been destroyed. Each step of recall of the ECS means that a new transmission channel has been found and new MECs are being formulated.

Remember the patient will feel tortured, frustrated and very depressed and will have a very limited attention span. Frequent, simple and short reentrainment is best.

Focus

Revised 1/21/93

All of the hereditary MECs of the DNA are intact in the remaining living cells of the hemiplegic, but the biofeedback transmissions between the hereditary MECs and those of the acquired conditioned MECs in the cell bodies have been capriciously damaged by the stroke. The channeling of these transmissions, prior to the stroke, represent thousands of the repetitive stimuli through a lifetime and are relatively rigid. A classic example of this is a child learning the complicated programming for walking.

The reentrainment of this programming will require integration of new transmission channels with those areas of the brain unaffected by the stroke. It is conjectured that this can be done in an accelerated manner by using stimuli intensities, durations, timing and repetition to formulate new conditioned MECs along new lines of biofeedback transmission.

Reentrainment Measures For Survival Instincts

Item 1. Rewards and/or Punishments for accomplishment and/or failure to carry out commands or requests. Rewards in the form of praise, treats, stroking or grooming. Video replays of the patient's progress through the treatments. Punishments in the form of scolding or stepping away from the hands-on position being used and, as a last resort, stimulation by applied electrodes. Repetition of these entrainment measures within the attention span and tolerance of the patient.

Item 2. Involve the patient in his favorite pastimes prior to stroke, such as special music, reading of favorite subjects, trips in the car, visits to friends, shopping malls, church, sightseeing, travel, circus, movies, etc.

Item 3. Requires presenting the stimuli of favorite foods.

Item 4. Present food menus verbally, or visually printed, or pictured on a television screen, or movies of someone eating; monitored by electrical sensors.

Item 5. Electrodes on those muscles selected to carry out commands or requests for a specific function. Stimulation of the muscles following a warning. Commands and requests presented visually as printed words, orally and/or with passive movements through the desired exercise range. External stimuli can be tried on a trial and error basis, varying in intensity, duration, timing and repetition.

Reentrainment Measures For Reproductive Instincts

Item 6. Erotic stimulation of the patient by any means in an attempt to reach intact areas of the brain so important in the total personality and brain function MECs. Might help to have the wife or girlfriend indulge in sexual foreplay using encouraging words and actions of reward.

Item 7. Encouraging hereditary emotions of pride, ego, loving responses to others, kindness to the attendants, etc.

Item 8. Conversation by close members of the family of the problems of maintaining the home, providing financial planning and any wishes of the patients in the future welfare of the offspring, provided some acknowledgment system can be achieved.

The series of 5, "Mapping the Mind," in the September-October 1993 issues of the *Wall Street Journal* are powerful stimuli that demonstrate and illustrate the controlling role of emotions in brain-cell functions. The series open vast vistas into cellular metabolism, applicable to the cells of the brain, body and all living organisms. The two basic emotions of survival and reproduction, are the stimuli that "produce temporary increases of physiological activity in an organism or in any of its parts," without which all living organisms would have become extinct. All of the millions of emotions, that evolved thereafter, are derivatives of these two.

In every phase of the "Mapping the Mind" series, it is the emotion stimuli which produce and create the response results described. All of the authors cite the many ways in which "motor control networks reroute stimuli in minutes;" "more than triple the size of the motor maps;" "reassigned control of her left-arm extensions from its old spot on her stroke damaged right brain, shifting it all the way over to her brain's left side;" catching a fly ball is not an inborn talent. It is like crawling and walking, it is a motor skill that must be learned and improves with practice."

Dr. Lisberger says "we've come up with where the learning occurs. Now we're asking how?"

Learning is the accumulation, storage, recall and processing of memories. These memories are called MECs or Memory-Emotion-Concepts; a new theory of brain-cell functions.

The mechanics of how we learn is the core of this theory. In the primordial ooze the emotions (Survival and Reproduction) evolved neuropeptide stimuli which combined with the receptors found in every living organism cell. These neuropeptides were catalyzed by the receptors into MECs and stored as the engrams of knowledge for that cell. This was the first of three steps of learning, leading to thoughts, decisions, actions and decisions.

LEARNING-EXPERIENCE-MOTIVATION

Learning is acquired by hard work and repetition, not by osmosis. Experience is a process of trial and error. Motivation is a God-given drive (hereditary?) to succeed especially with the inspiration and encouragement from parents, friends and strangers, as well as, the stimuli encountered from one's environment from conception, throughout life.

Rewards and Punishments are two powerful emotions for learning.

It is hypothesized that emotions (MECs) can create and re-route communications between cells. This will require an Emotion Profile for any given person. Hopefully the emotions that grow and restore the neural network bridges between the intact islands of nerve cells of the hemiplegic and quadriplegic will be found.

MECs are the result of millions of years of evolution; they may be subliminal, subconscious, or conscious but always involuntary. They will make brain and body cell research a precise science.

Thoughts On Stimuli That Direct The Non-Volitional Processing In The Brain

Benjamin Libet, University of California - San Francisco, established that brain activity precedes voluntary acts, followed by conscious decisions to act, followed by the acts.

First: Stimuli will have intensity, duration of action, repetition and timing. Stimuli may be extra or intra-cellular in origin.

Second: Cells respond in many ways and along many routes. The brain contains 10 to 100 billion neurons, each of which receives stimuli through 1,000 to 100,000 dendrites sending responses through their axones to other cells. All body cells inter-communicate through the neural networks.

Third: Cells have receiving and/or perceiving mechanisms for stimuli, called receptors.

Fourth: Neuropeptide stimuli that interact with the receptors are comparable to specific keys fitting specific locks.

Fifth: Interaction between a receptor and a neuropeptide is called catalysis. Neither is changed during the interactions, which will be consistent each time.

Sixth: When neuropeptide stimuli are catalyzed by the receptors, the response molecules are called MECs having EMFs and PS with the potentials to Excite (+) and/or Inhibit (-) the metabolic equilibrium of the organism.

Seventh: All of the MECs constitute the sum of the knowledge of that organism.

Eighth: A Definition of Emotions illustrates the role of total control they have of all organisms. "Emotions are a physiological departure from homeostasis that is subjectively experienced in strong feeling (love, hate, desire, fear, hunger, thirst, fatigue, etc.) and manifests itself in neuromuscular, respiratory, cardiovascular, hormonal and other bodily changes preparatory to overt acts which may or may not be performed."

Ninth: The MECs resulting from the catalysis of the neuropeptide stimuli by the cell receptors are stored in memory, recallable by stimuli. One familiar type of recall is the immune response in allergies. The antigens are the neuropeptide stimuli, the MECs are the memory of the allergic status and catalysis induces the responses of urticaria, antibodies, anaphylactic shock, et al.

Tenth: When stimuli recall a MECs, the responses are chain reaction biofeedbacks and parallel processes through the neural networks. There is a second intercellular communication system called psychoneuroimmunology via the vascular, neural and lymphatic channels.

Recalled MECs. Intense stimuli and strong MECs provide rapid recall. Old non-reinforced MECs may take longer or be lost temporarily or forever.

Eleventh: Parallel processing is a biofeedback stimulation of memories in processing centers for survival and reproduction. For example, when an antelope sees a lion charging, there is an instant recall of the Lion memory. The memory recognizes the threat to life. Parallel processing leads to simultaneous stimulation of many systems: Flight entails coordinated muscle actions; increased heart rate and faster breathing; selection of a course away from the lion's path; choosing a speed to exceed that of the lion; to name but a few.

A conditioned reflex is another example of parallel processing. The sights, smells, tastes and sounds of food stimulate the flow of stomach secretions. Pavlov's dog acquired a learned conditioned reflex, with repeated bell-ringing simultaneous with food-serving. The bell sound alone was able to produce the secretions after many trials and errors.

Dr. Allman at Caltech describes processing centers or "maps" that coordinate multiple systems of visual function. He found individual retinal cells for motion, shape and color, etc. He believes the neocortex has myriads of sensory maps, such as touch, hearing, speech, movement, etc.

Does the one-celled paramecium have "maps?" It would seem reasonable that it does. The sensory system of the paramecium consist of a receptor window, "the excitable membrane," and the "neural tube."

When the paramecium collides with a wall, the impact stimuli is catalyzed into a response of reverse swimming. This is followed quickly by a response of turning 45 degrees to one side and then swimming forward again, free of the wall. This would be a hereditarily-acquired conditioned reflex.

If the paramecium can acquire environmentally conditioned reflexes, which are learning, it is humbling and awesome to think that decisions, actions and creations have been developed for millions of years, in a one-celled organism, and that man is just one of the top rungs of the evolutionary ladder.

This brings up the question of whether mankind has "Will Power and Won't Power" or is he like a toy monkey who runs up and down the pulled string as his emotions dictate.

If Mankind Has No Volition And Is Merely Reacting To His Emotions, then we must find those emotions that will "open his eyes that he may see; open his ears that he may hear," and give him the tongue that he may speak.

This will be a difficult concept for mankind to accept, but if he wants truth, he must agree and he will find that after due contemplation he has been controlled and ruled by his emotions all his life, like it or not. Realistically, nothing has changed in his responses to life's emotion - stimuli from the beginning of time.

THE SIMPLEST DESCRIPTIONS OF BRAIN AND BODY CELL FUNCTIONS

1. Neuropeptide stimuli coalesce with the receptors that are a part of every cell, producing responses, called (MECs) or memory-emotion-concepts.

2. Neuropeptides are created by mechanical, chemical or emotional stimuli. For examples; A burn from a hot stove creates the neuropeptides which, in turn, create the MECs of pain (mechanical): poison-ivy toxins create the neuropeptides in the skin cells and recall the programming of allergies with blisters, itching and redness (chemical): a loved one dies and the grief creates the neuropeptides causing crying and tears: or a comedian tells a humorous story that creates the neuropeptides leading to laughter (emotion).

3. Neuropeptides are catalyzed by the receptors into MECs which are the engrams of knowledge and the programming of that cell.

4. MECs can be the acquired programming, resulting from the stimuli of the environment, starting the moment of conception.

5. Programming is modified and blended throughout life.

6. MECs are the currency of our bank of knowledge.

7. When the currency is deposited, similar to knowledge, or withdrawn, it can only be accessed by an account number. The account number is the stimulus that opens the ledger for deposit or withdrawal.

8. When one wishes to deposit or withdraw the MECs from the brain or body cells, the stimulus or (account number) calls for a review of the stored information, liked the bank balance, from which the information is to be requested.

9. The review scans all the stored MECs programming and recalls or withdraws the information to be recalled. This information represents short or long-term memories as well as the most recent or the most intense memories.

10. This scanning review is the first step of the thinking process and is called Propagation of emotion memories. Propagation consists of chain reaction biofeedbacks and parallel processings. Each step of propagation creates an increase in the bank balance of New MECs. This is how our MECs are modified and accumulated throughout our life. See "Rosetta Magnets."

11. Body cells have similar responses to stimuli. Poison-ivy toxin is a good comparison. When the toxin is catalyzed by the skin receptors the programming of the sensitized cell is recalled and the responses are activated in the decisions, actions and creations for blebs, itching and redness.

Memory-Emotion Concepts (MECs)
-Their Creation And Dynamics-

DEFINITION: "Emotions are a physiological departure from homeostasis that is subjectively experienced in strong (?) feelings (love, hate, desire, fear, hunger, thirst, fatigue, etc.) and manifest themselves in neuromuscular, respiratory, cardiovascular, hormonal and other bodily changes preparatory to overt acts which may or may not be performed."

1. Homeostasis evolved to insure Survival and Reproduction.

2. Emotions are stimuli to the cell receptors or MECs found in all cells, establishing and maintaining homeostasis by catalyzing neuropeptide stimuli into responses.

3. Emotions are the stored memories of cells, reflecting the responses to stimuli from all hereditary and acquired experiences. They are called Memory-Emotion-Concepts, (MECs).

The (MECs) are more than memories but also the receptors that catalyze recall neuropeptide stimuli into new (MECs) responses. The recall process initiates the biofeedback chain reactions and parallel processings through centers, called maps, leading to new (MECs).

Dr. Allman, at Caltech, describes processing centers or "maps" that coordinate multiple systems of visual function.

One cell dealing with motion, another with shape and another with color, etc. He has also found evidence of myriad maps that parallel process intracellular interactions throughout the body.

EXAMPLE; The antelope must see, recognize and remember the danger of the charging lion. Some of the antelope's decisions are; instant flight, entailing coordinated muscle actions; faster heart and breathing rates; an escape route; maximum speed and evasive maneuvers.

The recall of the (MECs) may be conscious, subconscious, but never voluntary. The chain reaction feedbacks and the parallel processings of recall and thinking will continue until the Electromotive Forces and Polarities are exhausted and the New MECs become the father of our thoughts.

Thoughts are the involuntary summation of all stimuli and responses, unique for each individual and original creations of one person's brain.

The involuntary and original summation of stimuli - catalysis-responses will create decisions and actions, thereby completing the cycle of a cellular and/or brain function. It is hoped that these concepts will nullify the cherished myths that man controls his own destiny.

These concepts may make artificial intelligence accessible and make rehabilitation of the hemiplegic feasible.

Criminal acts will be recognized as the results of a lifetime of anti-social conditioning. Criminals may be stimulated by neuropeptides that will catalyze MECs compatible with society or, if intractable, swift capital punishment be meted out for the common good, relieving the ever-mounting over-crowding and costly maintenance of the jails.

Alcoholism, smoking, drug addition, obesity and many habits are examples of emotions out of control; divorce and angers are classic emotional forces precipitating foolish decisions; wars, strikes and riots occur and succeed when we listen to or read inflammatory opinions by outside stimuli.

Salesmen and advertising of all kinds feed on man's emotional vanities, egos, desires, lusts and greed. Married couples and their children learn early what emotional strings to pull to gain their objectives. The family pet knows the master's weaknesses.

All Emotion concepts (MECs) are complex arrays of hereditary and acquired programs derived from stimuli from external and internal origins by the processes or propagation, discrimination and summation, (defined elsewhere), as well as, by feedback through a myriad of channels to a myriad of centers.

Pavlov's demonstration, of salivation in the dog when a bell sounded, is a conditioned reflex whereby the perception of the salivation stimuli will temporarily substitute for the real salivation stimuli reception.

In the same way all our MECs, which are synonymous with memories or education, can be stimulated by sights, sounds, tastes, touches or smells, which are perceived as alternates for the real original stimuli reception for the programming.

These programmed conditionings by perceived stimuli will become Extinct without periodic re-enforcement by the original stimuli.

Extinction of conditioning is synonymous with memory loss. It is a blessing in times of grief, humiliation, costly errors in judgment, fears, worries, etc. It can be a curse as one grows older.

Conditioning programming of MECs comprise the bulk of our memories and engrams of education. An example might be our basic Christmas tree. Until the tree is adorned with ornaments, tinsel, lights and the electricity is turned on, we have a simple tree, the basic MECs program. In full regalia, our perception is a thing of beauty and, then, attrition sets in with burned out bulbs, falling ornaments, etc. Too much decorating and the basic tree is obscured, such as hatefully contested divorce where the marriage vows are erased.

The cells of the body have a different form of perception as compared to the central nervous system, where stimulation of our senses initiates the conditioning. An example would be a skin cell with a highly reactive basic MECs to poison ivy toxin.

In some cases this immunity is permanent and in some cases of allergy the antibody antigen must be periodically injected, because of extinction.

How The Brain Cells And Neurons Construct And Combine The Stimuli They Receive Into The Responses We Call, Memory-Emotion-Concepts (MECs), Which Can Be Stored, Recalled, Modified And Then Restored

This is how we learn to think, decide, act and create. The sum of our MECs is the sum of our learning. It is an involuntary function, whether conscious or subconscious. All MECs learning is the sum of the emotions of the stimuli and it is the sum of those emotions that create the responses.

We will use the multi-faceted word "Hat" as an example. A hat has many characteristics, such as material, color, usage, style, cost, source of supply, texture, smell, taste, size.

Each of these are catalogued MECs for their individual characteristics and these are further catalogued down into their molecular aggregates which are subject to recall, modification and restorage by appropriate neuropeptides.

What do we know about Material? Is it felt, straw, cloth, paper, plastic (hard or soft), etc. with which most of us are familiar, according to our past experiences and contacts.

Each facet of the subject material is filed away in some of the billions of brain neurons, undoubtedly in different cells in different people.

As rainfall on a mountain top courses down to the plains forming streams and rivers to end in lakes and oceans, so will the diverse paths of neuron stimulation and learning end up in underground pools and rivers of learning in the depths of our brains. Memory recall is like casting a net to capture the fish in a certain area, plentiful when we are young but meager as we grow older.

Color? Each of us interprets color, based on the rods and cones of our vision. Even though each individual has their own interpretation, the use of universal terms in our language allows our brain cells to communicate with other brains.

Usage! There are hundreds of variations of activities with special requirements for hats. Our interpretations of hat usage will be entirely dependent on our experiences.

Style! These vary from generation to generation and from one person to another. The appeals of one style over another will be dependent on all the hats seen in a lifetime, whether on another person, in a movie or picture or perhaps some individual vanity when seeing ourselves in a mirror.

Cost and Supply! This will depend on the intensity of our desires and vanities; our frugality or lavish frame of mind and finding a source for purchase of a hat, which may be entirely dependent on accessibility and the effort required to find it, but mostly, on the intensity of our desires.

Texture! Stiff or pliable? Hats can be folded or crumpled but will they shed rain and protect against ultraviolet rays?

Smell! Dependent on one's sweat or the odors in the work place, etc.

Taste! Dry and flat!

Size! We can eyeball a hat and judge from experience whether it would be too large or too small.

In summary, a Hat has a thousand nuances of appearances, uses, memories. Our personal wardrobes possess many types and varieties. Each of us will have personal likes and dislikes for Hats. Their MECs for hats will be the combined sum of all the stimuli up to the time a memory is recalled.

Each MECs we harbor in our brains; each response to any stimulus is stored in our brains, or in the case of plants, animals, birds, fish, or microorganisms in their cells as an item of learning.

In the grand scale of life they are created in response to the demands or the necessary insurance for Survival and Reproduction. All extinct species failed and who knows when it will be our turn.

MOTIVATION IS THE PRESERVATION AND REFLECTION OF THE PHENOMENAL SELF

This is not as iconoclastic as it might appear. Selfishness, pride, ego and aggression are necessities for survival. Unselfishness, humility, sharing and tolerance are necessities for reproduction.

A theory of brain function is presented to show how the emotion concepts above are woven into the fabric of education in each individual.

Emotion concepts are anatomical molecular configurations within every body cell. They are the engrams (units of education) capable of receiving and perceiving sensory stimuli and catalyzing them into motor responses. They are our memories which father our thoughts.

They are summations of the electromotive forces and polarities of the stimuli which inspire our memories, leading to thought.

We then have the motor responses of decisions, actions and creations.

Emotion concepts are formulated and modified throughout our lives by the stimuli intensities, durations, timing and repetition and the conditions of "How," "When," and "Where" at that moment. Concepts are uniquely individual.

To illustrate the magnitude of conceptual educational emotions, take the word "Hat." One might ask, "How can the word 'Hat' possibly be an emotion concept?"

Would your wife empower you to go out and buy her a hat? This would be absurd! Consider the tentacles associated with the concept "Hat." Material, cost, color, style, dress, occasion and trust in your judgment, to name but a few.

As you can deduce, this theory proposes that all human behavior is the motor response to the summation of all the electromotive forces and polarities of the stimuli we receive and perceive from our heredity and environment, catalyzed by our emotion concepts, MECs.

What takes place to initiate a train of thought, determine the paths of leading to the conclusion and/or overt actions; which may or may not be performed; of which we may be consciously aware or subconsciously unaware.

Thinking occurs in three steps: Propagation, Discrimination and Summation.

These steps may result from evolution or mutation. They are successful only as far as they insure survival and reproduction of the species. Acquired MECs result from in-utero and post-natal stimuli from the moment of conception until death.

It is hoped that these concepts will nullify the cherished myths that man controls his own destiny.

These guidelines may provide guidelines for "Accelerated Rehabilitation of the Hemiplegic," and open a new viewpoint on the formation, understanding and treatment of criminals, divorcees and war, etc.

Perhaps it will add a new understanding of advertising that feeds on man's emotional vanities, egos, desires, lusts and greed.

This is a hunting trip to target where an idea lurks in a cell; how it is born; what are its ingredients; how are they recalled, modified, restored; and how do they communicate within the cell or to other cells.

As described earlier, MECs are created when neuropeptide motor stimuli are catalyzed by the cell receptors into sensory responses.

This phenomenon might be likened to the explosion of responses that result when a finger touches a hot stove. The first catalysis by the touch sensor is the finger pain; the second is a message to the brain, with a reflex withdrawal of the finger. This is an inherited requirement for survival. The third catalysis creates and stores this Burn as a New MECs through parallel processing and chain reaction biofeedbacks via neural networks and the vascular and lymphatic channels of the Psychoneuroimmunology Systems creating intracellular communications between all cells involved.

This catalysis called "Hot Stove" is the first step of learning. The next question is "How do learned MECs, in a cell, blend or respond to an incoming new MECs?" It is estimated that each cell contains 6,000 atoms. This represents a multitude of combinations and permutations.

MECs are the catalytic responses to the neuropeptide motor stimuli received by the cell receptors. They are composites of all the catalyzed motor stimuli received in a lifetime. All the MECs comprise the extent of our learning. When articulated they create and display our thoughts but the vast majority are subliminal and subconscious.

AN EXPLANATION OF BRAIN AND CELL FUNCTIONS

PART 1

Every cell has a receptor, memory and a function, dependent on the structure in which it is located. Since the beginning of time, cells, and later the brain, have evolved strategies for survival and reproduction.

Cells must be capable of reception, storage, recall, modification of their information, plus restorage. These are required inherited and acquired abilities for all living creatures, whether man, animal, plant or micro-organism.

Cells must be capable of receiving sensory stimuli and processing motor responses to them. Sensory stimuli and their responses are emotions.

In all walks of life there is sensory information available to brain and body cells.

For mankind, the dictionary has many thousands of words, each one of which has an emotional interpretation. Musical scores are abundant in variety and infinite in the emotions they evoke.

Scenery, paintings and photographs may arouse pleasing or distasteful emotions. Books and poetry appeal to many emotions. Advertisers and politicians strive to sway our emotions to buy something or to vote for their candidate.

Wife and children, friends, associates and strangers all incite emotional exchanges. Every stimulus has an emotional appeal whether pleasurable or distasteful; to be accepted or rejected.

MECs are the emotions, residing in the cell receptors, where they can be recalled by appropriate neuropeptides.

Neuropeptides were originated by trial and error in the primordial ooze. They have the capacity of stimulating cell receptors to catalyze the motor responses of MECs. They are the keys that unlock and ignite the learning processes.

When MECs are recalled they may be modified, restored as New MECs and added to the learning stores in the cells of man, animals, plants or microorganisms.

PART 2

Brain and nerve functions begin when the receptors in the neurons receive sensory stimuli and produce motor responses. These molecular responses are the keys that open the doors to cell functions and learning processes. They are emotions, too.

Antigens are examples of molecular responses and are the "immunologic target molecules that signal the presence of an invader."

"Antigens are not merely pieces of a pathogen but often molecules constructed by the host's cells from bits of the pathogen's proteins and from cellular proteins called major histo-compatibility complex (MHC) molecules. The processing and assembly of antigens are the key to the flexibility, the specificity and the thoroughness of an immune response." These processes are learned functions.

"The processing of antigens is intimately tied to the mechanisms that synthesize and recycle all proteins inside cells and transport them between intracellular compartments."

"MHC molecules can bind to an extraordinarily diverse set of peptides. A human cell has between a half million and a million class

I molecules of a single form; we estimate those molecules present more than 10,000 different peptides and perhaps as many as 100,000."

"How Cells Process Antigens" by Dr. Victor H. Engelhard, *Scientific American*, August 1994.

We propose that MECs are molecules bound to "an extraordinarily diverse set of peptides" that enable cells to store, recall, transfer, modify and restore (information and learning). The significance of any MECs will be proportional to the percentages and intensities of their components of punishment and reward. They are non-volitional and not governed by reason and logic.

As examples, the sound and sight of an attacking wasp are indelibly imprinted in the MECs memory by its sting. Searing injuries and insults to our vanities are years in losing their painful memories. All MECs are engendered by emotions.

Mankind, generally, refuses or is afraid to accept that they really don't have will or won't power. This blow to man's omnipotence is a real barrier to understanding and accepting these ideas of brain cell functions. This blindfolds research.

TWO WAY LABYRINTH BETWEEN BRAIN AND BODY CELLS, LEADING TO THOUGHT PROCESSES, DECISIONS, ACTIONS AND CREATIONS

Thinking about Brain Function! Questions, queries and observations start one on a train of thought searching for the mysterious and intricate ways stimuli lead to memories, thoughts, actions, decisions and creations, through a labyrinth of many billions of neurons, nerve tracts and many nuclei.

The key theme is that Memory-Emotion-Concepts (MECs); alias Learning or Conditioning; are essential to receive and perceive the stimuli to which the brain and body are subjected. Stimuli may originate from two sources;

1. INTERNAL; The programmed memories, in the DNA, which control the autonomic functions of physiology, catalyze the sensory stimuli from physiologic changes in the body into motor responses which then act as stimuli to return the body to a state of equilibrium.

2. EXTERNAL; The continuously changing memories in the body cells, separate from the DNA, catalyze sensory stimuli into motor responses and, by chain feedback reactions, become sensory stimuli to other cells. The stimuli from both sources act in harmony

with each other and by a process of propagation, discrimination and summation the MECs are catalyzed into thoughts, decisions, actions and creations.

It is conjectured that two phenomena occur, when MECs receive or perceive sensory stimuli, motor responses results:
ONE: The electromotive forces (EMFs) and polarities (PS) of the sensory stimuli are catalyzed into new Motor Response MECs in the body cells, carrying out the programmed instructions of the DNA, for maintaining metabolic equilibrium.
TWO: The motor responses exiting the cells or the DNA (EMFs and PS), then assume the role of sensory stimuli to other cells in countless chain feedback reactions, through the processes of Biofeedback. This is the science of Psychoneuroimmunology, where all body cells, inter-connect through neural, vascular and lymphatic channels.

As the memory bank of engrams are being updated by the stimuli, they father Thoughts and summate into decisions, actions and creations. Thoughts with sufficient EMFs and PS intrude on our consciousness.

<u>The vast majority of thoughts are summated into subconscious decisions, actions and creations, of which we are completely unaware, but which, in turn, are summated into updated MECs, silently.</u>

WHAT IS CATALYSIS AND HOW DOES IT FUNCTION?

Catalysis:

"A separate force, especially one that is essentially unaltered by the reaction." The DNA in the ovum and in the sperm are classic examples of catalysis. When the two unite in fertilization, growth is precipitated, genes are exchanged but the programmed DNA remains intact and the programmed instructions of the genes create a uniquely new baby.

The memories of the DNA are unaltered but, with the new science of Biogenetics, they may be manipulated.

The catalysis that takes place in the interactions between the MECs of the body cells and the DNA, is illustrated in the definition of Emotions.

We conjecture that these body changes may be conscious or subconscious but are involuntary summations of the MECs forces. The stimuli affects will depend on the stimuli intensities, durations, timings and repetitions. The new science of Psychoneuroimmunology, with considerable evidence, postulates that body cell and DNA functions are coordinated. They consider this science as a Sixth Sense. This includes hormones, endocrines, immune responses, enkephalins, electrolyte regulation, etc.

A Cut In The Skin As An Example Of The Sixth Sense Function

The acts of healing are MECs-controlled. Stimuli (neuropeptides) from the wound mobilize the response forces of clotting, serum release, leukocyte transportation to the site, cellular growth and a signal to stop when the skin is healed, etc.

One-cell organisms, liked Paramecia can be conditioned, so they, too, have MECs. They both are subject to reinforcement, extinction, reward and punishment, etc. Memory-engrams (MECs) in the brain and body cells have the same properties.

An Attempt To Define The MECs In The Paramecium

It has been estimated that each cell contains 6,000 atoms, exclusive of the DNA. Each atom has a valence, "a degree of combining power," which this theory conjectures as electromotive forces (EMFs) and polarities (PS). The core of this theory is that the summated EMFs and PS of the 6,000 atoms will combine with the EMFs and PS of the stimuli being received and perceived by a cell through the dendrites of a neuron, as an example, and exiting through an axon as a motor response with specific EMFs and PS. In short, there is an exchange of EMFs and PS, with the atoms in the cell remaining but with an updated configuration which we can call MECs or Conditionings, a continuing process throughout life. The memory-engrams (ECS) of the DNA are physical-chemical entities and, likewise, the MECs of All Body Cells are physical-chemical entities.

The human brain with its billions of neurons, each with 10,000 synapses, have provided mankind the capability of survival and reproduction through the vicissitudes of the Unknowns to which our earth has been heir. To assist this capability, the more we understand about brain function the better we may fare. The human brain may provide mankind the capability of survival and reproduction through the changing Unknowns to which our earth will be subjected.

There are many moves possible; each move stimulates a counter move response by the adversary. When a MECs is recalled it is interpreted by all the changes since it was first stored. The interpretation of the opponent's moves determines your next move. A Win, Loss, or Stalemate is the Sum of All Moves Before. MECs are Emotions.

MECs responses result when neuropeptide stimuli are catalyzed by the cells. MECs reflect the cell programs evolved through evolution and environment. MECs responses create New MECs, just like a move of the chess pieces will alter the game plan. When the MECs catalyze stimuli, the responses, through biofeedback chain reactions, will affect all future functions. These are the distilled sum of all the MECs programs within the body.

When the MECs (Hat) is recalled, propagation produces many memories, such as; size, shape, material, color, cost, occasions for its use, etc. The word "Hat" may be spoken, written, heard and a hat can be touched, visualized, smelled and tasted. The MECs is multifaceted as a memory.

Discrimination is the selection or rejection of the "Exciting or Inhibiting" stimuli. EXAMPLE; What color "Hat" shall I buy;' to wear with what dress; for which occasion; and will the budget permit it?

Summation is the bottom line of the EMFs (Electro-motive forces) and the PS (Polarities), resulting from propagation and discrimination. EXAMPLE; My MECs "Hat," at this moment and in this store, bids me to buy that pink hat with the flowers on it. It will be very "Exciting" or pleasing with my new Easter outfit.

Propagation, discrimination and summation lead to the decision and action response; "Buy."

PARALLEL PROCESSING OF A MECs

The formulated MECs in memory will catalyze subsequent incoming stimuli into motor responses in four ways:

A. Genetic or hereditary MECs will catalyze the sensory stimuli of sight, sound, taste, smell, touch and position sense in a two-way feedback between brain and body as proposed by the Science of Pyschoneuroimmunology.

B. Genetic MECs will catalyze stimuli from the autonomic system.

C. Acquired or conditioned MECs will catalyze stimuli from the sensory system.

D. Acquired or conditioned MECs will catalyze stimuli from the autonomic nervous system.

The motor responses from these four types of catalysis, in a chain reaction, are now the sensory stimuli that formulate MECs throughout the body. Simultaneously, the two-way feedbacks are propagating, discriminating and summating into conscious or subconscious MECs that we consider to be thought, decisions, actions and creations.

CHRONOLOGY BY AGE GROUPINGS

MECs and their resultant Thoughts, Decision, Actions and Creations differ in proportion to the stimuli to which we are subjected through life.

We will consider how the MECs of Pain, evolve through the following age groups:

A. Under 3; With no prior MECs, a bee-sting simply means pain and an instinctive flight, crying and running to mother.

B. 3 to 12; Now the bee-sting MECs is identified by sound, sight, word, speech and hearing.

C. 12 to 20; The bee-sting MECs now incorporates the How, When, Where and What.

Anticipation and defensive action are a part of the MECs-Pain.

D. 20 to 45; The bee-sting MECs include the knowledge that anaphylactic shock can occur and the fears of multiple stings and killer bees have modified the MECs-Pain.

E. Over 45; The bee-sting ECS incorporates caution and avoidance of danger areas. Acceptance and or tolerance for the MECs-Pain become the conditioned motor response to the bee-sting stimuli.

APPLYING THE PRINCIPLES OF "LABYRINTH" AND "PAIN" TO FUTURE RESEARCH INTO BRAIN AND BODY BEHAVIOR.

1. A paper dealing with the Hemiplegic.

2. Criminal Justice that recognizes crime as an Involuntary Response of one's MECS and that reformulation of the criminals MECs may be the only way to prevent Recidivism.

3. How does our Religion and our fear of the Unknown affect the course of our lives?

4. Could these principles accelerate and expand our Educational Potentials?

5. Will our Survival and Reproduction be enhanced by applying these principles in the centuries ahead?

In conclusion, it is predicted that brain and body cell function will be substantiated along the principles outlined above.

Seventh Premise: The MECs in each cell is specific for that cell and the communicating channels it has evolved are also specific. Furthermore, the MECs, of the moment, change with each stimuli received and perceived and the catalyzed motor responses are unique creations of that cell only.

It is conjectured that the DNA of each cell functions like the brain of the CNS, conducting the performers to produce the harmonies of the composition.

Eighth Premise; If artificial intelligence is to duplicate the processes of brain function, it must duplicate the principles that govern a single cell.

Some of the requirements are:

1. Stimuli that can be received and perceived by the cell MECs with the correct EMFs and PS input to achieve the desired output.

2. The EMFs intensities and the PS of the stimuli must interact with those of the MECs and be catalyzed into the motor responses of decision, action and creation.

   a. When food is presented to the paramecium as rewarding, positive and exciting stimuli, it must respond with the decisions, actions and creations to move to the food, ingest and digest it, eliminate the by-products and determine when its hunger is satisfied.

   b. When a noxious substance appears in the environment, stimuli that are punishing, negative and inhibiting, the response decisions, actions and creations must move the cell out of harm's way or face death.

3. The principles are the same as we ascend the evolutionary ladder but, in place of the one-cell paramecium, we now have 100 billion neurons, 100 trillion connections and trillions (?) of body cells, communicating through neural networks back to the brain.

Ninth Premise; If we meet the requirements described above for artificial intelligence, we are, in essence, modifying human behavior.

To Modify Behavior with Artificial Intelligence, We Must:

1. Assign a numerical value to the EMFs and PS of the MECs of the individual who's behavior we propose to modify.

2. Assign numerical values to the stimuli selected to interact with the existing MECs, EMFs and PS, which will summate into a New MECs-memory-education and simultaneously, summate into decisions and/or actions and creations from the old MECs.

DNA-RNA DATA

It is interesting to speculate on the role environment plays in evolution.

Emotions are molecular configurations acting as catalysts, translating sensory stimuli into motor responses. Furthermore, Emotions are in a continuous condition of revision throughout life, summating those EMFs and PS derived from the stimuli of the environment and the stimuli derived from the DNA.

There are an estimated 3 billion base pair of genes in the DNA. Mendel's classic experiment with the fruit fly demonstrated that dominant and recessive genes would produce a predictable mathematical percentage and the offspring.

These percentages were gene changes in the DNA.

We already know that drugs given to a pregnant woman will result in various anomalies and deformities in the offspring, e.g. thalidomide. These were mutations in the genes of the DNA of the developing embryo. Carcinogens are another example of mutations in the DNA which led to the development of cancer, in various types of body cells.

Both of these examples illustrate the ability of environmental stimuli to mutate the DNA. For mutation to take place in the DNA, it is conjectured that the stimuli must have penetrated the cell membrane and interacted with the cell cytoplasm before reaching the DNA in the nucleus.

For the mutation to interact, the stimuli from the DNA must be transmitted through the cytoplasm to cells outside. This indicates that mutational effects are a total cell effort.

Recent studies of the translucent round worm, C. Elegans, has demonstrated that destruction of specific genes arrests certain developmental changes, thereby producing a reverse mutation, which may explain some of evolution's variations.

It is conjectured that our day-to-day environmental stimuli may lead to infinitesimal mutations of which we are unaware.

One of the startling phenomena of modern society is the marked increase in the average height of mankind. It is unlikely that physical activity is a factor as society is far more sedentary now than before. One must consider vitamins, but the poorer segments of society share in the increased height but probably have few vitamins. Balanced diet appears to be the same. Soft drinks with their added sugar or sweeteners, so prevalent today, may be a factor. Perhaps, climate, barometric pressures, cosmic rays, ozone concentrations, carbondioxide, pollens and industrial air contamination are implicated.

In conclusion, we can say that environmental stimuli in summation with the stimuli from the hereditary genes of the DNA may lead to predictable mathematical changes in the offspring, when we can better identify the genes involved.

This is an added dimension to Darwin's theory as an explanation for the changes that have taken place through the millenniums. It is hard to rely on Darwin's theory as the sole explanation for the infinitesimal variations of nature.

DNA MAP

1. Each human cell has 23 pairs of chromosomes.
2. Chromosomes are made up of DNA or deoxyribonucleic acid.
3. The DNA contains 100,000 genes.
4. Genes consist of "base pairs."
5. There are 3,000,000,000 base pairs.
6. Base pairs are composed of two of four basic chemical subunits; Adenine, Thymine, Guanine and Cytosine.
7. These basic chemical subunits code 20 amino acids.
8. These amino acids make up the different proteins that serve as the chemical basis for all living things.

LEARNING

Exciting MECs are security, self-assurance and happiness, versus inhibiting MECs like insecurity, uncertainty and sadness.

MECs were and are created when cell receptors catalyze neuropeptide stimuli from external or internal origins.

They are the programming and knowledge in each cell. Each cell contains 6,000 atoms with 100,000 genes and 3 billion base pairs, creating infinite combinations and permutations.

This file will refer to the creation and role MECs play through the following age groups: 1. The first year; 2. 1-5 years; 3. 6-14 years; 4. 15-21 years; 5. 22-35 years; 6. 36-60 years; 7. 61 years till death.

For simplicity, we will confine our explanations to the MECs of security, self-assurance and happiness as "exciting and rewarding" for homeostasis and metabolic equilibrium. The "inhibiting and punishing" MECs emotions will be insecurity, uncertainty and sadness.

1. The first year: The responses to stimuli in the newborn are dictated by the limbic system with little input from the brain. The limbic system controls the metabolic equilibrium of the cardiovascular, respiratory, digestive and endocrine systems, and allows a brain-dead person to continue living in the vegetative state with no effect on security, self-assurance and happiness. When the infant is hungry, dirty, wet, cold, hot or tired, etc., the mother soon learns to recognize the signs. She will cuddle, feed and change the diapers at least 20 times a day. There will be 7,300 such stimuli in one year to create and reinforce the exciting and rewarding emotions.

Each stimuli will have intensity, duration, timing and repetition, primarily in the subconscious and subliminal areas.

Now add the stimuli from the father, siblings, friends, grandparents, doctors and nurses as exciting rewards. Also digestible food and good sleeping habits contribute to the metabolic equilibrium of the infant. Exciting and/or inhibiting stimuli will constantly assail the infant in the first year. No wonder each individual has a unique set of emotions created by and reactions to his environment. This represents the normal acquisition of the exciting-reward MECs.

Next, consider the unwed mother who has few maternal instincts and is too immature to cope with the demands of a crying, hungry, dirty baby. This is the origin for the inhibiting MECs of insecurity, uncertainty and sadness. No MECs of an infant can be understood without some understanding of the emotion profiles of the infant's mother and father and their experiences as children.

2. 1 to 5 years: This is a period of expanding exposure to stimuli from outside the home and is critical to the child's development. Reading is a powerful influence for learning, especially in later years, as well as a potent influence in preparing the foundations of security, self-assurance and happiness, that will last throughout a lifetime. The MECs will be proportional to the stimuli intensities, repetitions, timing and durations.

Walking, talking and the imagination are vividly expanding at this age. Learning is by leaps and bounds, with excitement and rewards spurring higher and higher achievements. Severe inhibitions and punishments may lead to cessation of learning. This age will be very sensitive to ridicule and criticism, and may intensify insecurity, uncertainty and sadness. Child care facilities, if properly directed, can do much to counter these harmful MECs.

This is the "What's for Me" stage that may elicit temper tantrums along the way. Manipulation of parents and siblings is common. Sharing and cooperation need to be taught. Sharing and accepting occasional game losses will depend on the parent or teachers. Most children in this period have no aversion to cheating in order to win. Encouragement and love will offset insecurity, uncertainty and sadness.

3. 6 to 14 years: The home is slowly replaced by peer activities but will remain as the port in the storm in troubled times; a place for food and sleep; and a source of love bolstering self-confidence. They seek adventure and excitement outside the home. Peer pressure is high and often leads to family disputes and rebellion against the rules of the home. The school takes up the majority of the day's time and the ties to the home get weaker. Chores are easily forgotten. Parents are bypassed until there is an important favor needed.

Interest in the opposite sex awakens. Participation in school activities, sports, games take precedence over cleaning one's room or performing home chores. The inhibiting emotions of insecurity, uncertainty and sadness are fostered by poor grades, obesity, pimples, lack of a close friendship or even ridicule or imagined rejection by one's peers. The difference between perception and/or rejection by others is important and needs all the skills of a parent to reaffirm the child's worth.

4. 15 to 21 years: The apron strings are almost severed. Independence, conceit and over-confidence are the rules of the day. Driving a car becomes a real worry for the parent. Drugs, drinking and sex become something the parent can only guess about unless it confronts them. Choosing a wrong role model will drive a parent up the wall. This age is mostly deaf to advice from the parent and tends to defy the customs of their elders.

Parents hope and pray for someone to "light their lamps" as described by Admiral Rickover. Curiously, the child emerges unscathed by all the dangers along the path and the parents can take a deep breath after its all over. By now the exciting an rewarding MECs of security, self-assurance and happiness are pretty well established. For an unfortunate few, the inhibiting and punishing MECs of insecurity, uncertainty and sadness will mold and direct the course of their lives.

5. 22-35 years: By now the shape of one's career is outlined. Education is almost over; job and career have begun. The majority will get married, otherwise a mutual agreement to share an apartment is worked out. There is little commitment binding these relationships. Each partner having a career delays the start of a family and puts stumbling blocks in the path of sharing life together. There is reluctance to commit oneself to another. The bonds of sex and personal commitment are easily broken. Since little is put into the agreement, the need to consider the partner's wishes and desires are minimal.

Religion is not a major force unless children are born, when a whole new universe opens up and parents plunge wholeheartedly into the children's ethical teaching. Marriage partners will ask themselves, "What did we used to do before our children completely monopolized our lives?" The marriage takes on a new meaning. All plans of life revolve around the children. Parenthood leads to nurturing and teaching the children to succeed and be happy in life.

Security, self-assurance and happiness are the rewards for a successful launching of the children. Should the children need help over some of the obstacles in their lives, parents can lend a helping hand to offset the children's insecurity, uncertainty and sadness.

6. 36-60 years: The children are shortly to strike out into the world on their own. Home and work will change very little. Vacations are family affairs. Retirements and pensions become the order of the day. With luck, no major medical problems exist for the family. Mother and father are drawn close together and their concern for each other becomes a very prominent part of life. Finance problems have been stabilized. Buying a new car brightens the days and makes trips for the family a fun adventure. These are mellow times. If the MECs were rewarding and exciting, it will be a pleasant time of life. If the MECs were inhibiting and punishing, one must grin and bear it.

7. 61 years to the end of time: Hobbies, home and garden, clubs, parties, receiving old friends as guests or visiting old friends and relatives and, of course, visits to the children and grandchildren. Mother and father become very solicitous of the health and welfare of each other. "Bringing in the sheaves" is the reward for an unselfish and thoughtful way of life dedicated to security, self-assurance and happiness. Wishing and complaining are the roles of insecurity, uncertainty and sadness.

These thoughts are the mirrored reflection of one man and one woman's life and are designed to smooth the highway of life for our grandchildren, and to provide steady and pleasant breezes to sail their ship of life into safe harbors. We've seen our children run the course but their genes and MECs are like their parents, some good and some not so good.

The accompanying poem about the man in the glass, may help.

THE MAN IN THE GLASS

When you get what you want in your struggle for self

And the world makes you King for a day,

Just go to the mirror and look at yourself

And see what that man has to say.

For it isn't your father, mother or wife

Whose judgment upon you must pass,

The fellow who counts most in your life

Is the one standing back from the glass.

You may be like Jack Horner and chisel a plum

And think you're a wonderful guy,

But the man in the glass says you're only a bum

If you can't look him straight in the eye.

For he's the fellow to please - never mind all the rest

For he's with you clear to the end.

And you've passed your most difficult test

If the man in the glass is your friend.

You may fool the whole world down the pathway of years

And get pats on the back as you pass.

But your final reward will be heartache and tears

If you've cheated the Man in the Glass.

The limbic system evolved as the original responses to insure survival and reproduction of any species.

The long-term responses, mainly directed at preservation of the individual, included searching for and securing food and drink, and fight or flight responses to danger.

Other responses are for reproduction; including mating, rearing of young, home building and other forms of social behaviour. The limbic structures are also intimately involved in emotional behaviour, both in terms of subjective feelings such as fear, rage, pleasure, etc., and in the objective physical expression of these states.

Finally, the limbic system evolved memory patterns for survival and reproduction which are passed on to offsprings.

Comparative zoology tells us that a fertilized egg develops into a mature organism, according to the evolved programming of its DNA.

When a newborn human baby arrives in the world, the limbic system already has the capability to maintain life. This is the system that permits the human to survive on a life-support system when the patient is brain-dead.

Function of the mid- and fore-brain begins at birth, when subjected to stimuli from the environment. The infant is born with the ability to perceive (recognize), receive and react to sensory stimuli from his external environment and from the internal metabolic requirements.

Perceiving, receiving and reacting are illustrated by the biofeedback chain reactions and parallel processings of the antelope in a migrating herd. The antelope must perceive that the lion following the herd is at a safe distance, no response necessary. Suddenly the lion charges and perception, reception and escape responses are necessary, if it is to survive.

This tableau is a replica of the beginning of function of the mid- and fore-brain in the infant. All of the sensory stimuli, which the infant will perceive, receive and react, will determine his education. Education is the combined sum of all the forces of sensory stimulation harmonized with the hereditary forces of the limbic system.

As an example: A foreign language cannot be learned without perceiving, receiving and reacting to a course of internal and external sensory training. Every facet of memory and thought will lead to motor responses to these stimuli.

Consider the newborn, complete with a hereditary reflex limbic system developed to preserve survival and reproduction. Brain and body cell functions of decisions, actions and creations are derived from the environmental stimuli, from the moment of conception on. This is the first step of learning and education.

The sensory stimuli, beginning at the time of birth, will be exciting and inhibiting. Education begins with these stimuli. When stimuli impinge on the sensory systems, the emotions they evoke are either original or summated with the previously-stored memories. If the stimuli are identical, the emotions are potentiated. This we call Proliferation or the first facet of education.

However, if the stimuli are somewhat different, then the MECs are modified into a somewhat different molecular configuration, again, dependent on the EMF and polarity being summated. This modification will be exciting for homeostasis or inhibiting. This we call Discrimination and/or a decision. This is the second facet of education.

The third facet of education is the Summation of the electromotive forces and polarities of propagation and discrimination.

WISDOM IS THE INTELLIGENT APPLICATION OF LEARNING

Survival and reproduction of any organism was and is proof of its learning. "Learning is the acquisition and/or selection of existing knowledge."

What Exactly is learning? When sensory stimuli react with cell receptors there are motor responses. If stimuli can "incite to activity" then the cell's responses had already been learned. Learned responses evolved from inherited or acquired sources. These responses evolved from inherited or acquired sources. These responses are physical entities, unique for that individual, and form the cell's knowledge and programming.

The cell's motor responses to stimuli not only include the learning but the emotional significance of that learning. Every stimulus received by a cell will be "exciting" and rewarding for that cell's metabolic equilibrium or "inhibiting" and punishing. Emotions are the cloaks that envelope our learning. Learning and emotion change from moment to moment and from individual to individual. Emotions are the physical entities or molecular configurations that carry memories and the programs within each cell of our bodies. They are the Memory-Emotion-Concepts, referred to hereafter as the MECs.

All emotions are derived from survival, which is the instinct emotion of an individual, and reproduction, which is the instinct emotion of sharing, parenting and dependence between people. Without these two all life would be extinct.

MECs were "hatched" in the primordial soup, by trial and error, billions of years ago, creating the forerunners of all the species living today.

It is conjectured that the first creations of living organisms, be they plant, animal or microorganisms would be the simple single cell, such as the paramecium or the worm C. Elegans. (More about the paramecium, later.)

Single and multi-celled organisms, if they are to succeed, must be capable of Survival and Reproduction. The requirement for survival is:

The capability to receive stimuli and to discriminate between those that enhance metabolic equilibrium (Exciting) or threaten equilibrium (Inhibiting). Through trial and error the exciting stimuli will reward skills for survival and encourage repetition and learning, while inhibiting stimuli will stop the trying and delay learning.

Exciting and rewarding stimuli accelerate metabolism and cell activities, not the least of which is the intensity and range of learning.

Returning to the primordial soup, the mother of our lives, she has devised some very ingenious maneuvers over millions of years.

She has devised neuropeptide stimuli, which are the neuromodulators in the nervous system and the hormones in the endocrine systems.

Once the role of emotions is accepted, research can concentrate on emotion profiles for individuals, groups, nations, etc. Geoffrey E. Hinton, *Scientific American*, September 1992, page 145, "How Neural Networks Learn from Experience" describes the hidden weights. Devoid of Will or Won't Power!

Learning and knowledge are the MECs in each cell. They are the programming for that cell, whether it is a nerve cell in the brain or a muscle, fat, skin cell, etc., of the body. Every cell of the body is in communication with every other cell through neural networks and the vascular and lymphatic channels of the science of Psychoneuroimmunology. Their functions are similar for all organisms, one or multicellular. Man, animals and plants all function with the MECs evolved through trial and error over millenniums of time with the goal of survival and reproduction for any one species.

RESEARCH SUPPORTIVE OF THESE THEORIES

Thomas Cech, University of Colorado, and Sidney Altman, Yale University, shared a Nobel Prize in 1989 for their discovery of an enzyme with catalytic action in ribonucleic acid.

This enzyme, called a "ribozyme," is capable of storing information and of self-replication. They speculate this may explain the beginning of life. They believe it may open vistas of viral manipulations, including AIDS.

The catalytic action of ribozymes may be the beginning of the stimuli-catalysis-response of MECs. Memories, recalls, chain-reaction feedbacks, parallel-processing, conditioned-reflexes, etc.

MEMORY-EMOTION CONCEPTS APPLIED IN
ACCELERATED REHABILITATION OF THE HEMIPLEGIC

Brain injuries are the unpredictable and bizarre interruption of the normal stimuli-catalysis-responses learned through a lifetime. Nerve pathways and exchange nuclei centers are destroyed and the patient is unable to tap or communicate with his stores of accumulated knowledge.

It is proposed to create a new repertoire of MECs, incorporating memories from the undamaged areas left after the stroke where possible.

PROBLEM; Imprisonment of the hemiplegic within his own body is "Living Hell." The total dependence of the hemiplegic on his family or on society is "Soul Destroying." The financial drain is enormous. Salvage of these mentally normal derelicts is the ultimate in humanitarianism.

PREMISE; The majority of stroke patients have an intact opposite cerebral hemisphere, which they are unable to utilize after a lifetime of entrainment and channeling through the corpus calosum to the damaged hemisphere.

HYPOTHESIS

Accelerated and concentrated reenactment of the stages and steps of learning can restore the hemiplegic to a self-sufficient state quickly and economically.

PRINCIPALS INVOLVED

Stimuli should aid and abet survival, reproduction and homeostasis. Rewards for responding to command stimuli will be more effective than punishment. However, patients who are very despondent, pessimistic or stubborn may require some mild form of punishment.

Stimuli should be aimed at propagation of biofeedback chain reactions and parallel processing. Stimuli should be chosen on the basis of discrimination between exciting or inhibiting and how the patient is receiving or perceiving that stimuli.

Choosing the most effective stimuli will require the wisdom of a Solomon. An emotion profile of the patient may be obtained by attaching instruments to the patient that will monitor responses, such as pulse rate, blood pressure, pupil diameters, sweat, saliva, stomach acid, body postures, facial expressions, etc.

The next step is to stimulate the patient by questions, commands, approvals, pleading, scolding, scorn, humor, kindness, etc. One of the most effective stimuli will be "hands on" caressing, stroking, squeezing, loving or sexually arousing, and maybe mildly painful, like an electric shock. Group rehabilitation may help, but is not as personal.

All rehabilitation training should take place without distractions. Most patients will have a short attention span.

Normal feedbacks from the normal limbs may override the training stimuli. This can be prevented by immobilizing the normal limbs as he sits in a chair. A darkened room may help for some stimuli.

The patient should have electrodes applied to the skin over the muscle groups selected for the training. Stoelting Company of Chicago has a programming machine for patterned electrical stimulation (PES) which has had some success in the hands of Dr. Kroll, professor of exercise science, University of Massachusetts. Dr. Kroll would not start treatment until a year had passed. This may lead to disabilities from disuse, and delay would seem unwise. Dr. Kroll limited his treatments to every one to two days.

I am reminded of the total knee replacements at the Mayo Clinic where the patient was placed on a continuous flexion-extension machine on return from surgery. Patients were walking in three days. Accelerated rehabilitation requires immediate and continuous therapy, up to the point of intolerance. I can not imagine any deleterious effects that immediate therapy might have on the brain as compared to the advantages of establishing mental templates for the muscle movements chosen at once.

It is impressive that an unconscious child will respond to its mother's voice but not to that of a stranger.

Instructions and commands to be given by trained personnel or a very close and loving relative who is willing to follow orders.

Commands can be given on a VCR with explicit instructions on what will happen and what response the patient should make as demonstrated on the movie.

Also VCR films before, during and after therapy to be used as teaching aids to the patient and as rewards for any progress accomplished. Review may be very encouraging for the patient.

Commands to be very simple in the beginning. Progressing as improvements occur.

When a command is given and not followed, a warning buzzer sounds. Failure to respond is promptly followed by an electric stimulus, intensity to be determined. Prompt timing is very important in a learning exercise. Any slight movement and the electric stimulus is switched off by the therapist.

Spontaneous movement will automatically switch off the electrical prod. Commands can be given at frequent intervals (like every 15 minutes) or as determined by trial, as long as the patient doesn't cry or become agitated, at which point, therapy is stopped temporarily. Negative reinforcement will cancel progress.

Between therapies the patient can be transported to super marts, malls, flower gardens, restaurants, familiar places, etc. Favorite music is an aid, as are family get-togethers and plenty of recounting memorable events in the patient's past. Reading to the patient and television watching will help.

Asking advice of the patient, as he improves, is a great morale builder.

Plenty of pep-talks with the theme, "Freedom from Dependence on Others is in Sight."

Do not permit the patient to become a hypochondriac, or to expect to be continuously waited upon.

Many things may be done if ingenuity is used. Love is probably the strongest reward of all but should never diminish the patient's self-respect and independence or permit guilt ... all the trouble he's causing. Nor can he transfer responsibility for poor performance on to the therapists, or, specially, wife or daughter.

When one considers the hundreds of thousands of trials to learn to walk or to talk, it is apparent that accelerated retraining of the hemiplegic may require the patience of a saint.

Dr. Candace Pert, chief of brain biochemistry, N.I.H., is one of the pioneers of psychoneuroimmunology and in the foreground of brain research.

Reference to *Whole Earth Review*, page 106, summer 1988, "The Material Basis of Emotions."

QUERY

How do brain and/or body cells acquire information?

Is this process restricted to the kingdom of mankind and animals?

What of the remaining four kingdoms of plants, fungi, protists and monera (including bacteria and blue-green algae)?

These five kingdoms over eons of time have adapted to changes in their environment.

Is there a common denominator that applies to these changes in all five kingdoms?

The common denominator could be defined as learning.

WHAT ARE THE REQUIREMENTS FOR LEARNING?

1. Receptors to receive motor stimuli from external or internal sources, probably neuropeptides, were evolved since the beginning of time.

2. Every stimuli has an emotional component which will excite and/or inhibit the physiological equilibrium of any cell.

3. The sensory responses to motor stimuli are the keys to cell equilibrium.

4. We suggest these sensory responses be called Memory-Emotion-Concepts, or MECs for short.

5. MECs have the unique capacity to be stored in cells, recalled, modified, and restored as expanded learning.

6. MECs make learning possible and confer on any cell of any kingdom the quality of decision making, acting and creation of responses.

7. They are called thoughts in the more evolved organisms and responses in the more primitive cells.

HYPNOSIS OR EMOTIONS VERSUS "WILL OR WON'T POWER"

When a person can walk on hot coals without apparent pain or can raise the temperature of a body part by increasing the heart rate and blood flow to that part, is it an act of "will or won't power?" Is it a learned emotion response to sensory stimuli, such as self-hypnosis or cataplexy?

Hypnosis defined: "a state induced by the suggestions and operations of the hypnotist with whom the subject remains in rapport and responsive to his suggestions, which may induce anesthesia, blindness, hallucinations and paralysis."

Cataplexy defined: "sudden loss of muscle power in animals and man following a strong emotional stimulus (as fright, anger or shock) characterized by clear consciousness but loss of muscular control." I once witnessed a small bird hypnotized or catalplexed by a snake in that same bush. It was paralyzed.

When in Jamaica, some years ago, I witnessed a religious ceremonial dance where natives became increasingly agitated until they fell down in a trance. Perhaps it was mob hysteria, somewhat like the lemmings and whales committing suicide; maybe drug-induced; or a form of cataplexy.

Intense concentration on a body part or telergy to distant receptors in other people's minds, makes one wonder if parapsychology could be a factor. Financial wizards and con artists have the ability to predict or anticipate the emotions in the minds of potential buyers.

It is a fact that a person can walk on hot coals and can control the sympathetic and parasympathetic body responses to increase the blood flow to an extremity. To do this, one must receive or perceive stimuli sufficiently powerful to block or erase feelings of pain. To deliver warming blood to a cold extremity one must focus and concentrate on imagining the memories learned and recalled of how a warm body part fells. The act of calling on the heart to speed up and increase output is a lot like focusing on a 3-D picture and concentrating until each eye calls up its own vision. This might be classed as a mild form of self-hypnosis or splitting stimuli to different areas of the brain or body.

Examples of sufficiently powerful stimuli to block or erase normal common-sense reactions and reason, are:

Intense anger provoking an attack on someone stronger and bigger; patriotic fervor of the Kamikaze pilots diving to their death; gambling into the poor house; spending into bankruptcy; greed turning into stealing; ego-maniac like Hussein in Iraq, bankrupting his country; Hitler trying to conquer the world and exterminating Jews; over-powering craving of the obese, chocoholics, alcoholics, drug addicts; smoking despite emphysema. These emotion stimuli appear to be self-hypnotic.

Obviously, powerful emotions: such as anger or hate, greed, lust, craving, ego, pride, vanity, selfishness, etc., can stimulate some bizarre responses when they are catalyzed into MECs.

Perhaps self-hypnosis can create the emotions required to walk on hot coals and deliver warm blood to a cold extremity.

There are many self-hypnosis or mob-hysteria phenomena, such as; burning witches at the stake; Crusaders slaughtering people in the name of Christ; mob hysterias of lynching, looting and vandalizing; revolutions and sit-in protests; the mass panic in escaping a burning building; the list is endless. There is a strong admonition from a father to his children as they leave home to enter the world: "Never do anything in a crowd that you would be ashamed to do alone." This is the parent's prayer "I hope the temptations (emotions) of the world will not be strong enough to hypnotize you."

Hypnotic or hysterical acts are initiated by emotional stimuli by external forces. Self-hypnotic acts require stimuli from the internal emotions of the MECs. These acts may be conscious or subconscious but, in the final analysis will always be involuntary. They are not acts of "will or won't power!"

ENGRAMS

Engrams are units of education, emotion concepts (MECs), and atomic-molecular configurations, within all the cells. They are re-structured by the incoming environmental sensory stimuli in contrast to hereditary programs of DNA and RNA within the cell nucleus, which are unaffected by sensory stimuli other than mutation or recombinant techniques.

Reviewing life's experiences, I remember the exciting, pleasant, humorous and stimulating emotion concepts. All but the most un-pleasant and intense inhibiting concepts soon fade away. They are counter-productive for survival and reproduction.

Fear, pain, worry, hate, anger, shame, greed, vanity, cowardice, infidelity, insecurity, criticisms, punishments, weaknesses, failures, lies, debts, loneliness, dependence, laziness, crying, poorness, dis-trust, lust, sadness, etc. are concepts soon forgotten. These are Inhibiting (-) for Survival and Reproduction. They are threatening to homeostasis and result in actions and counter-measures to escape, justify, rationalize and forget.

The hereditary instinct concepts of the DNA and RNA are permanently in cell memory unaffected by the day-to-day emotions.

On the other hand, confidence, pleasure, security, love, flat-tery, unselfishness, humility, bravery, fidelity, self-confidence, praise, rewards, strengths, successes, truth, solvency, companionship, inde-pendence, ambition, laughing, richness, trust and happiness, etc., are remembered and savored.

These are Exciting (+) for Survival and/or Reproduction. "They enhance and preserve my phenomenal self," not only for myself but also for the reproduction of myself. They enhance homeostasis.

These Exciting memories warm us at the stove on a cold winter's night, warding off the chills of a threatening and alien world outside.

The old Indian belief that the strength of a conquered enemy becomes that of the victor, indicates that the Emotion Concepts That are Inhibiting will lose some of their EMFs, while the Emotion Concepts Exciting will increase their EMFs.

The corollary of these axioms is that Exciting Emotion Concepts— The Engrams of Education in Memory — can be enhanced by Sensory Stimuli that are Exciting. Conversely, Inhibiting Emotion Concepts — in Memory — can be diminished by Sensory Stimuli That are Inhibiting.

Advertising, raising a family and school education are, primarily, Exciting Sensory Stimuli. They demonstrate that more flies are caught with sugar than with vinegar.

APPLICATION OF THESE PRINCIPLES TO MODIFY BEHAVIOUR

1. Establish an emotion concept profile to determine which concepts are inhibiting to survival and reproduction, which are inhibiting to homeostasis and which are inhibiting to the culture of the society involved in the project.

2. Determine the degree to which the concepts are inhibiting.

3. Profile the exciting concepts and their degree to enhance survival and reproduction, homeostasis and social culture.

4. Devise Sensory Stimuli with sufficient intensity, duration, timing and repetition to diminish or eliminate Inhibiting Concepts and augment or create Exciting Concepts.

FEAR/LOVE

"Psychological and psychophysiological responses to threat or danger, accompanied by heightened autonomic activity."

Fears, real or imagined, are one of the most powerful stimuli in the formation of MECs. The MECs of fears may be acquired or hereditarily-learned conditioned reflexes.

The recall of the MECs-Fear initiates the steps required for survival of the species. When neuropeptides recall stimuli interact with the receptors of the Fear-MECs, the catalysis creates New-MECs which are the first link in the chain reaction biofeedback responses of recalled memories. This chain reaction will continue until recall stimuli lose their potential or until an elusive memory is recalled.

As well as recalling short- and long-term memories, there are the stimuli that are catalyzed into parallel processing responses in centers or "maps." Dr. Allman of Caltech discovered cell maps in the retina that responded to color, motion, shape or all. He cites myriads of brain sensory maps providing the stimuli for parallel processing, which are essential for specie survival.

Fears may be exciting (EX) or inhibiting (IN) or a combination. Fears can upset metabolic equilibrium and the compensating responses induced will be proportional to the intensity, repetition, timing and duration of the stimuli.

Fears are learned conditioned reflexes to punishments. The antonym of fear is Love and pleasure. Pleasures are learned conditioned reflexes in response to reward stimuli. Punishments and rewards are the backbone of learning.

If punishments are associated with pain, it is postulated that the MECs responses will have greater electromotive forces (EMFs) than rewards and be the dominant forces in learning.

A whip teaches more than a carrot for the donkey. Survival and reproduction would be impossible without punishments and rewards. Maintaining metabolic equilibrium is the price of survival and reproduction. The significance of any MECs will be proportional to the percentages and intensities of their components of punishment and reward.

MECs are non-volitional and, contrary to common beliefs, not governed by reason and logic. In the design of Artificial Intelligence programs (AI) to mimic the human nervous system these percentages and intensities will be the key factors.

Yes, Maybe or No responses from AI programming will depend on the exciting, inhibiting or neutral summations of the punishing or rewarding stimuli intensities.

Whether it will be a program for a single individual or a program for the majority of people will depend on the commonality of the emotions.

Can artificial intelligence be programmed to recognize danger or a problem, initiate escape from one and solutions for the other? Will AI learn from mistakes or become more consistent with repeated correct responses?

If a robot is programmed to make decisions on various problems, the problems would be designed so that answers will be choices dependent on the fears and punishments versus the pleasures and rewards that are input with the programming.

Would AI give decisions and answers that are true, false or mixed?

Many people cannot recognize truth, lies or wishes.

One step might be to list all the degrees and types of punishments that induce fears. We are all alike and our learning has been acquired along the same pathways but with different intensities and emphasis.

Love Data

The sermon by Dr. Fesmire today raised some queries of how to define the emotion Love. How did it evolve? When did it evolve? Is it altruistic? Does it occur in mankind solely? Is it restricted to those who believe in Christianity, etc.? What about pagans?

This chapter refers to altruistic love, not hormone-induced physical love. This is the type of love that was evolved to insure the survival of any species by sharing and creating in the thousand and one ways that mutually benefit the individuals, couples, herds, flocks, bacterial and plant colonies and the different races of all kinds.

It all began in the primordial soup eons ago. The original microorganisms sought and shared a compatible environment that was within the requirements and restrictions of their own metabolisms.

In order to survive, these primitive organisms acquired specialized traits that enabled them to reproduce, grow and adapt to the conditions in which they existed.

Prolific reproduction may have exceeded the destruction from adverse environments and enemies.

Along the path of evolution, mutations of genes occurred, producing individuals and/or species that could adjust to adverse environments or enemies. Extinction of the species was the price of maladjustment.

Adjustments were and are created by stimuli that produce the required responses necessary for life, which are gene mutations, coupled with many trials and error, and dependent on stimuli intensities, repetitions, timings and durations.

The stimuli that were evolved by these forces of nature, were probably neuropeptides that combined with the receptors found in every living cell. The neuropeptides were catalyzed, stored and recalled as MECs, among which was the emotion Love.

Love appears to be a God-given quality that was created to insure the survival of cells and assures their metabolic equilibrium. It requires no rewards or punishments in the learning processes as required for most emotions. However, the peace and tranquillity passeth all understanding.

Reward Or Punishment

Comparing reward and punishment in their ability to formulate emotion concepts, also known as engrams.

Instincts for survival and reproduction have evolved through sensory stimuli creating the motor responses which promote homeostasis and maintain equilibrium. These stimuli we consider as exciting (EX). Stimuli, which disturb homeostasis and disrupt equilibrium, we consider inhibiting (IN).

Training a newborn baby or a puppy are good illustrations of these stimuli. The cry of a hungry or wet baby prompts sensory stimuli to his caretaker, requesting food or a dry diaper. The whine or restless behavior of the puppy prompts food and/or a walk outdoors to relieve his bladder of bowels. Praise and petting reinforce these (EX) stimuli. Scolding, ignoring or punishing introduce (IN) stimuli. If the EX electromotive forces (EMFs) and polarity exceed the IN forces, memory-emotion concepts (MECs) become constructive and good for homeostasis and equilibrium — the goal we wish to attain. On the other hand, summated forces of inhibition will upset homeostasis and equilibrium — a goal not wanted. The creation and formation of MECs will be a blend of the EX and IN forces.

There are some age-old sayings; Success breeds success, failure leads to failure; Practice makes perfect; Habits result from repetition.

Consequently, sensory stimuli that reward, if strong enough, repeated often enough, timed appropriately and of sufficient duration, will formulate MECs that achieve our goals and provide a happy and stable newborn or puppy. conversely, stimuli with strong EMFs of punishment, will produce unhappiness, irritability, rebellion and anti-social behavior.

Examples Of Emotion Concept Modification In A Lifetime

Father is tying his small son's shoelaces when the son says, "I can do it." "Try it," says father. Failure in this and in many experiences through life are sensory stimuli which modify his self-image of infallibility. This is an emotion concept modification.

Simultaneously he is creating emotions of humility, establishing a diminished self-confidence and caution about trying new ventures. Carried to an extreme, he may become so inhibited he will be insecure and fearful. On the other hand, excessive praise and help from father may create an obnoxious, rude and arrogant child. The observation here is that, no matter how trivial our actions in life are, the emotion concepts (engrams) resulting, are woven into exceedingly complex patterns, which will direct our motor responses in speech, body posture, actions, decisions, etc. throughout life. Another observation is that computers designed to emulate the brain must incorporate the ability of continuously reprogramming themselves — a tall order.

I was fined $25 for speeding, one block from my home. This fine was a strong sensory stimuli, catalyzed by my emotions of chagrin and foolish waste of money into a motor response of caution. I drove lawfully in that area in the next few months. Gradually, my emotion of daring exceeded my caution and my motor response was to speed once again, but with one eye in the rear-view mirror. This is a classic example of my daring and independence emotions being modified and then slowing reverting back to the original state. This is equivalent to recidivism of a prisoner in jail.

Our 14-year-old dog died after years of mutual love and affection. Dying was a powerful sensory stimuli, catalyzed by death or fear of the unknown into a response of grief. Many daily incidents were stimuli recalling all the happy associated memories of our faithful friend. The avalanche of sensory stimuli that bombard us each day of life, slowly eroded or modified our grief, leaving fond but sad memories. Grief has added a new dimension and joins our ever-growing repertoire of emotion concepts.

Body cells can display emotion concept modification. When I was younger my skin was hypersensitive to poison ivy and for many years my summer were a torture of lotions, etc. Poison ivy was the sensory stimuli catalyzed by my genetic emotions of sensitivity, leading to rash, itch, blisters and oozing skin as the motor responses. Repeated stimuli exposure modified my sensitivity into a permanent immunity, which allows direct contact without any skin response.

I trained a young filly to respond to a lunge line and to voice commands to walk, trot, gallop or stop. The natural instinct emotions of the filly were to do and go where she pleased, when she pleased.

Winning her trust, plus a liberal application of rewards as sensory stimuli, I patiently modified these instincts into motor responses of compliance with my wishes. Repetition, timing and duration of the stimuli were prime factors in achieving this. Compliance became the new emotion concept, transforming her into a well-behaved mare. Without reinforcing training and turning her loose in the pasture for many years, she would probably revert to her natural traits.

NATURAL MODELS

NATURE

The recent discovery of the Supernova Shelton raises some philosophical musings of the nature of the universe, the nature of man and an attempt to understand the roles the mind and body play in man's behaviour.

The first conjecture is the presence of a supreme being, which we call God. The next conjecture, within the scope of man's knowledge, is that God created the universe with a plan that included the evolution of man.

The supernova is postulated to have formed the atoms and all the subatomic parts identified to date, illustrating the processes which could have led to life here on earth.

Initially, life consisted of one-cell organisms such as bacteria and the well-known paramecium.

These one-celled organisms are conjectured to have survived and reproduced or became extinct based on their adaptation hereditarily and environmentally to the conditions in which they existed.

It is conjectured that survival and reproduction are possible only if the organisms can receive and perceive sensory stimuli and catalyze them into acceptable motor responses.

As an example, the gonococcus bacteria were able to receive and perceive penicillin and die in the early days of medical treatment. However, the bacteria were able to catalyze the stimulus of penicillin into a defense mechanism response, insuring their survival.

It is important to understand the principles involved in this event as later applications to the brain-body functions will show identical processes. The penicillin is the stimulus and the surface of the Gonococcus is the hereditary receptor-perceiver. Initially, the penicillin overwhelmed the catalyst within the cell and the cell died. As time went on, some of the Gonococci were able to develop catalytic concepts blocking the toxic effects of the drug, enabling the bacteria to multiply. This is comparable to the antibody catalysts children develop after inoculations and to catalytic concepts adults use in immunizing themselves to cope with devastating events in their lives.

The paramecium is a one-celled organism that can receive and perceive the stimuli of its environment and catalyze the discriminating responses that reject the inimical factors in its environment and accept those factors that insure survival and reproduction.

These two examples, the responses of the Gonococcus and the paramecium to stimuli, represent the simplest forms of conditioning. These catalytic actions are the basic building blocks of evolution.

In the examples of the paramecium, the stimuli being received and perceived through the sensory surface will be "good" or "bad" for its survival and reproduction. The paramecium, being higher on the evolutionary ladder, has a limited mobility, permitting it to retreat from the bad and advance toward the good. The hereditary catalytic concept within the cell will electrically summate the electromotive forces (EMFs) and polarities (PS) of the sensory stimuli received and perceived which inhibit or excite the cell and catalyze a motor response toward or away from the source stimuli.

This is the basic principle found in the human brain-body which we call discriminating decisions leading to actions and creations. The responses made by the paramecium will be determined by the catalyst concept, which we refer to as memory, synonymous with knowledge and education in the human. Memories go through constant revision throughout our lives, depending on the hereditary and environmental stimuli we receive. They may be conscious or subconscious but will determine our thoughts, decisions, actions and creations.

We will attempt to show that all human behavior is predicated on the simple principle that stimuli received and perceived are catalyzed into motor responses in an infinitely complicated orchestration between mind, nervous system and body.

The relatively new science of psychoneuroimmunology recognizes this intimate correlation. The stimuli from the environment or from heredity, alone or in coordination, and enhanced by the biofeedback chain reactions and parallel processing, result in the variegated responses.

These variegated responses are the propagation, discrimination and summation of our brain's thinking processes leading to our thoughts, decisions, actions and creations.

This is a replica of the internal mechanics of any and all body cells and applies to all cells of the five kingdoms known to man. These are non-volitional responses, of course.

PAVLOV'S DOG'S RESPONSE TO A BELL

The dog's responses to stimuli of sight, smell and taste are acquired evolutionary learnings or conditionings for survival, called MECs knowledge.

The recall of these MECs becomes the stimuli for the reflex stimulation of stomach secretions. This is a chain reaction biofeedback.

THE MECHANISM OF A CONDITIONED REFLEX
(OR PARALLEL PROCESSING)

Whenever stimuli are simultaneously associated with other stimuli, as the sound of a bell in this case, the catalysis by the receptors will create new MECs whose molecular structures incorporate responses to both stimuli.

Touching a red-hot stove or associating the warning buzz of a bee-sting produces Instant MECs.

TWO FACES

1. "What I am!" or "What's for me?" insures Survival. These are laws of the jungle instincts.

2. "What I appear to be!" or "What's for you?" These are laws of the social instincts. To get you must give. This insures reproduction.

Every individual is a composite summation of his Memory-Emotion-Concepts or MECs. Understanding these instincts help solve the problems of groups and individuals; in families and schools; in the community and work force; in the nations and the world at large.

These faces may be expressed in body posture, voice tones, word choices, facial expressions and a multitude of autonomic nervous system reactions such as eating, flushing, rapid pulse, blood pressure changes, diarrhea, frequent urination, changes in pupil diameters, anger or irritability, sadness or happiness and many others. These are primarily involuntary responses and a reflection of the underlying emotions.

WE CAN ONLY BE AS HAPPY OR SAD AS OUR MECs DICTATE

Dr. Robert S. Elliot, director of Life Stress Simulation Laboratory, University of Nebraska, Omaha, has pioneered the stress responses to stimuli, calling them the "visceral-vascular readiness for combat or flight" people, pinpointing them as the "hot reactors," who may be in danger of physiological catastrophes. Their reactions are involuntary.

Examples of the hot reactors are found in both categories of the "two faces," such as: the vaunting ambition of emperors and kings to create empires; unquenchable greed to make money; incompatible marriages; promiscuity and teenage pregnancy; drug addiction; homosexuality; rapists, murders; etc.

Dr. Elliot identifies the 'hot reactor" and applies external entrainment forces to neutralize or erase the MECs that produced deficit reactions. He uses sensory organ approaches with neuropeptides such as endorphins, enkephalins, drugs, personal counseling, electrical and mechanical aids and expects to modify the MECs.

EVOLVE

When you swat a mosquito, stinging and sucking blood from your arm, you are reacting to a command evolved in your body millions of years ago.

Your ancestors would never have survived without this ability to react to stimuli, and storing and recalling the learning it would require.

All this is possible by the evolvement of several steps and requirements of the five kingdoms of nature, e.g. animals, plants, fungi, protists and monera.

The requirements were;
1. Evolve neuropeptide stimuli and,
2. Receptors in cells to receive them.
3. Catalysis of the stimuli into responses by the receptors.
4. Ability to store, recall, modify and restore these responses.

Undoubtedly this required umpteen years, many trials and errors and many more modifications to come.

One might question the above requirements for all the members of the five kingdoms, some of which may never have been studied with that much objectivity, especially monera that lack organized, condensed nuclei.

The protists like paramecia have been studied the most thoroughly and will be assumed to speak for the other living kingdoms. This may be a difficult stand to defend.

Paramecia fulfill the requirements mentioned above.

This exhibit is designed to show that one-cell organisms like the paramecium have the ability to metabolize, learn, store, recall and process information into decisions and actions, similar to neurons of the brain and body cells.

They also acquire conditioned reflexes.

This would indicate that brain-like functions as described above reside in each and every cell. These abilities were established billions of years ago. The paramecium is a one-cell organism that lives on wilted lettuce. It eats food and excretes the waste. It is capable of swimming in search of food and swimming away from noxious substances. It reproduces by asexual binary fission.

The ability to receive and perceive stimuli and react with responses is an inherited programming of all cells.

When the stimuli have sufficient intensity, duration, timing and repetition the responses are stored as memories. When stimuli activate memories the responses are recalls.

Activation or recall of memories starts a biofeedback chain reaction and parallel processing stimulation of other memories. This is propagation of ideas, one step in processing information. All recall responses will have "exciting or inhibiting" effects for or against homeostasis. Homeostasis assures survival and reproduction and prevents extinction of the species.

Determining if the effects are exciting or inhibiting is discrimination, another step in processing information.

Propagation and discrimination are non-volitional acts. If the effect is favorable for homeostasis, the paramecium will decide and act to go to the stimuli (food for example), and if inhibiting (a harmful substance), the cell will decide and act to retreat. Exciting and inhibiting stimuli have electromotive forces (EMFs) and polarities (PS). When the sum total of the EMFs and PS of propagation and discrimination are summated, the summation will be the decision to go to or retreat from the stimuli. Carrying out the decision is the action.

A CONDITIONED REFLEX IN THE PARAMECIUM

The goal is to demonstrate a conditioned reflex in a one-cell protist, the paramecium. The problem is to determine the capacities or lack of capacities of a paramecium, compared to a more evolved animal such as man.

Defining A Conditioned Reflex

Pavlov discovered that the ringing of a bell could stimulate stomach secretions in the dog, after a training period where the bell is rung while the dog was seeing, smelling and tasting food. This is a conditioned reflex or an acquired learning response superimposed on hereditary learning responses that promoted survival and reproduction. The response of Pavlov's dog involves chain reaction feedbacks and parallel processings, explained later.

The dog's response to stimuli of sight, smell and taste, evolutionary learnings or conditionings for survival, are called MECs or engrams of knowledge.

The Mechanics Of A Conditioned Reflex

The recall of MECs become New MECs which are the stimuli for the reflex stomach secretions.

Whenever stimuli are simultaneously associated with other stimuli, the sound of a bell in this case, the catalysis by the receptors will create New MECs whose molecules are structured to incorporate responses to both stimuli. The pain of touching a red-hot stove or the warning buzz associated with a bee-sting produces an immediate conditioned reflex.

1. Does a paramecium have a stimuli-catalysis-response capability? 2. Does it have a memory? 3. Can it recall a memory? 4. Can it perform chain reaction feedbacks and parallel processing? The answers are Yes.

Paramecium do have stimuli-catalysis-responses: A paramecium running into an object will back off, turn at an angle, and proceed forward again; or, if the polarity of the paramecium is reversed, it will reverse directions.

They have memory and recall when they are stimulated with food and will swim to it. They will move away from some chemicals and be attracted to others.

The paramecium is a one-cell organism, with a receptor window, excitable membrane and a neural tube. Chain reaction feedbacks and parallel processings in a paramecium are restricted to that single cell.

The mechanics of the chain reaction feedbacks, in the paramecium are the transfer of the electromotive forces (EMFs) and polarities (PS) of the stimuli into response EMFs and PS in the neural tube. The polarity of the neural tube and the intensities of the electromotive forces will determine the type of paramecium response and its direction.

Parallel processing in the paramecium would take place in the neural tube, which corresponds to the processing centers of multicellular organisms. When stimuli are catalyzed into responses in the neural tube, we already know that the paramecium is capable of coordinated and simultaneous responses to stimuli, as witnessed by the reverse swimming when meeting an obstruction, then turning on an angle and then forward swimming to escape. It is conjectured that there are receptors in the neural tube, at various levels, which will catalyze responses to the regions controlling reverse swimming, turning, and then forward swimming, all determined by the EMFs and PS of the stimuli-catalysis-responses. These are learned hereditary reflex responses.

A comparison to parallel processings in the neural tube would be a multi-outlet extension cord, which will activate all the outlets when plugged into a receptacle. This would be the stimuli-catalysis-response of the receptors in the excitable membrane. Each accessory plugged into the outlet will be activated, corresponding to the retreat, turn and advance of the paramecium on contact with an obstruction.

Van Wagentonk determined that acquired learned responses and conditioned reflexes in the paramecium were subject to extinction in 15 to 30 minutes. They will disappear in 30 minutes or less, unless reinforced by repeated stimuli.

DEMONSTRATION OF AN ACQUIRED LEARNED RESPONSE

The paramecium has an inherited and evolved excitable membrane which is a receptor and catalyst for receiving or perceiving the exciting or inhibiting stimuli in its environment, e.g. electrical, chemical, light, heat, "avoiding reaction," etc. The excitable membrane is comparable to the dog's senses of sight, taste, smell, hearing, etc. When the membrane detects, recognizes, or discriminates between exciting or inhibiting "obstacles or unfavorable" stimuli, paramecium will catalyze them into such responses as depolarization of the ciliary membrane and/or reverse swimming.

When the paramecium escapes a stimuli, it will resume its hyperpolarized state with forward swimming. This is the hereditary learned response of a paramecium.

INDUCING AN ACQUIRED LEARNED RESPONSE OR CONDITIONED REFLEX

If a paramecium is swimming in the direction of food and is electrically stimulated to reverse its swimming direction, simultaneous with turning on a light, over and over with various current intensities, timing, duration and repetition, and various types of light. It is hypothesized it will soon refuse to swim to the food. When the light only, is turned on and the paramecium reverses its swimming direction, one would have an acquired learned response that should persist for more than 15 minutes. It might be possible by varying the stimuli this could be improved to 30 minutes.

WHY IS A CONDITIONED REFLEX IN A PARAMECIUM IMPORTANT?

No. 1 Mankind is the evolutionary product of one-cell protists like the paramecium.

No. 2 The paramecium are molecular configurations with EMFs and PS, responsive to stimuli in their environment and to chemical changes internally. They have metabolism, growth, motility and reproduction as well.

No. 3 These capabilities are the hereditary learned responses and instinctual reflexes that characterize life.

No. 4 Demonstration of an acquired learned response and a memory provide the ingredients for a conditioned reflex.

No. 5 Conditioned reflexes in a paramecium are the progenitors of brain and central nervous system functions.

No. 6 Demonstration of a conditioned reflex establishes a continuous chain of evolution from a one-cell organism to mankind.

The optimal temperature for the highest rate of swimming, food intake, food-vacuole formation and the action of the contractile vacuoles was found to be between 22 and 26 degrees C. Learning consists of increased permeability of the cell membranes, a bioelectrical control, which gives the cell the avoiding reaction (AR) and swimming velocities.

The excitable ciliary membrane regulates the direction of the ciliary beat which then regulates the swimming behavior of paramecium.

It is held that the stimulations can be electrical, chemical or mechanical in origin and that paramecium membranes have the same basic properties as neurons, sensory cells and other excitable cells.

Learning in the paramecium begins with responses to stimuli, called taxes. Taxes maintain the orientation of the paramecium with respect to some directional stimulus. (Wichterman, 1986). Chemotaxis toward a chemical stimulus is positive and away negative. Geotaxis is in response to the earth's gravitational pull; Phototaxis to light; Thermotaxis to heat and cold; Thigmotaxis to mechanic contacts with hard surfaces; Barokinesis to hydrostatic pressures; Rheotaxis to water currents; Galvanotaxis to electrical currents; Ref.: Ralph Wichterman "The Biology of Paramecium."

This may seem unrelated to brain function and responses to stimuli, but is the simplest form of cell function and identical in principal to all the functions whether single or in the millions of cells in the human body.

Paramecium And A Single Cell

The design of this experiment is to stimulate the paramecium with light and/or heat, simultaneously with the stimulation of food; after a time one can omit the food and expect that heat and light will prompt it to move to the site where food was presented. This will be an acquired conditioned reflex, demonstrating that the one-celled organism, the paramecium, can react to stimuli; produce a response of learning or memory; which in turn can be recalled and processed into a decision; and then perform a learned reflex move to where the food stimuli had been but is now heat and/or light. This is a learned processing of information.

This experiment demonstrates that one-cell organisms like paramecium, have identical responses to stimuli as do the brain and body cells, namely:

1. With food as a stimuli, the response is to go to and/or receive food, eat, and digest it.

2. When noxious stimuli are presented, the response is to retreat from the irritating or harmful agents.

3. Each type of response requires a reception and/or perception of a stimuli.

4. The responses are stored as memories, an inherited learning capacity.

5. When stimuli prompt a recall of memories, associated and related memories respond in a chain reaction. This processing of memory information is propagation.

6. Recall memories can become stimuli by a feedback mechanism. This is the biofeedback chain reactions and parallel processings.

7. These stimuli of the recalled memories have exciting or inhibiting electromotive forces (EMFs) and polarities (PS) enhancing or threatening homeostasis, which insures survival, on the one hand, or extinction of the species on the other.

8. When the paramecium are stimulated by these recalled memories, they must discriminate if they are to survive.

9. Survival demands decision and actions. Decisions and actions follow the summation of the EMFs and PS of propagation and discrimination.

10. These stimuli response programs are being continuously modified and updated throughout the lifetime of paramecium, brain or body cells.

11. Acquired programming will disappear by extinction if not periodically reinforced by stimuli. Examples are the loss of memory without reinforcement; loss of immunity to antigens in allergic cells, without booster shots.

12. In conclusion; the stimuli-response mechanisms of the paramecium are identical to those of the brain neurons and the body cells. Paramecium can memorize (learn), store, recall, and process information into decisions and actions.

This means that evolution has programmed every living cell to survive as well as reproduce for billions of years.

CORRESPONDENCE AND READINGS

NEWSWEEK

Reading "Mapping the Brain" in the April 20, 1992, issue of *Newsweek* and the scientific pioneering into the brain's "fixed hardware" is most interesting. The anatomy and circuitry of the brain are unbelievably complicated.

We offer an explanation of how brain and body cells receive and/or perceive neuropeptide stimuli in their receptors.

The stimuli are catalyzed into responses, which can be called MECs. These are stored as the beginning of learning.

When MECs are recalled by neuropeptide stimuli, they initiate chain reaction biofeedbacks and parallel processings through the neural network channels.

There is another communication network channel that connects every cell of the body with every other cell of the body through the lymphatic, vascular and neural channels of the Psycho-Neuro-Immunology Systems.

These two channels make possible Thinking, Deciding, Acting and Creating.

Neuropeptides are critical to nerve and brain cell functions.

SOME PERSONAL CONCLUSIONS, AFTER 20 YEARS

1. The 100 billion neurons and the billions of body cells are inextricably intertwined and must be considered together in any study of learning processes.

2. Each neuron and each body cell have receptors that were evolved from hereditary stimuli over eons of time and are modified by environmental stimuli from the moment of conception.

3. Receptors are the keystones of the learning process. Receptors are called MECs. Each MECs is one of the millions of emotions to which the body is heir. Emotions are as complex as the billions of combinations and permutations of the atoms they contain.

The definition of emotions illustrates the vital role they play in cell functions:

4. For example: Someone slaps your face. This stimuli may release a flood of neuropeptides which are catalyzed into the emo-

tions of shock, anger, shame, humiliation, etc., and into responses of decisions, actions or creations as dictated by your lifetime of experiences at that point in time.

You might retaliate; turn the other cheek; ignore the incident; and/or apologize.

5. Emotions are not cognitive and volitional. They may be conscious but are primarily subconscious and subliminal.

They are like the pulled string that makes the monkey run up and down. There is neither Will or Won't Power.

6. A one-celled paramecium has a "window" receptor that translates neuropeptide stimuli into decisions, actions and creations unique for a particular stimulus and that one organism.

There is strong evidence that the paramecium can learn conditioned reflexes. It would also imply a single body cell that was stimulated by a poison-ivy toxin or was burned by a hot stove would decide that the insulating toxin was to be diluted by a blister in a response action or that the burned skin would turn red, blister or char as a defensive response. Both responses being unique creations of those cells.

These are non-volitional reactions.

7. The principles of accelerating rehabilitation of the hemiplegic could apply to behaviour modification of criminals; school children lacking motivation; marital disputes; international strife; etc.

8. Behavior modification has an ominous and odious connotation. But in our own homes, when we teach, scold or implore our children, we are attempting to modify behavior and influence their thoughts, decisions and acts.

In summary, "Accelerated Rehabilitation of the Hemiplegic" would be enhanced by pin-pointing the anatomical areas of functioning cells and rerouting the communication circuitry to them. Restoring function to these sites will require the stimulation of and the catalysis by the MECs. Response training programs mean long hours, much hard work, many trials and errors and lots of motivation.

Emotions that had a major role in the patient's life prior to his stroke would be effective. The results could be an earlier return to almost-normal living.

Dr. Dan W. Urry
Professor of Biochemistry, Physiology and Biophysics
Univ. of Alabama, Birmingham

Dear Dr. Urry:

Your article "Elastic Biomolecular Machines," *Scientific American*, January 1995, has "lit my lamp," as Admiral Rickover strove to do for his students.

Your article describes responses of biopolymers to the "inverse transition temperatures."

Permission is requested to plagiarize how the brain and nervous system respond to the "transition temperatures" of emotions to create what we term MECs, which are the foundation stones of learning and lead to thoughts, decisions, actions and creations.
A definition of emotions portrays the awesome influence they play in our lives.

MECs are the "elastic biomolecular machines" that natural selection has found over the course of three billion years.

To be more specific; they evolved in the primordial ooze when sensory stimuli neuropeptides were catalyzed by cell receptors into motor response antibodies. Reference: How Cells Process Antigens, *Scientific American*, August 1944.

MECs create the knowledge or programming in the cells.

They have the unique properties of being stored, subject to recall, modification and restorage as New MECs and additions to the bank of knowledge. For 30 years my thinking and writing has centered around,

"Accelerated Rehabilitation of the Hemiplegic," which presents more questions than answers but did lead to a theory of brain and cell functions.

There are many ways in which your article goes to the core of molecular interactions and which I am plagiarizing. Please let me know if I misconstrue.

"The natural selection of three billion years" supports the creation of ATP for your biomolecular machines, as well as the evolution of neuropeptide sensory stimuli catalyzing cell receptors into motor responses. The inverse temperature transitions for folding and unfolding biopolymers might be likened to the energies released by the MECs.

MECs are the learning and knowledge of each cell and combine to create the total knowledge of their host. They make thinking and thoughts possible in mankind.

All living organisms, such as the one-celled paramecium, demonstrate decision-making, taking action, and creating responses unique for that organism.

The intriguing stimuli of your article is the incisive approach to the core of molecular interactions, which open the doors to learning, recalling, thinking and creating at the molecular level.

The objective of this paper is: How do we recall, receive and send messages and commands from the brain or from a cell and to various parts of the body? How do we recall and review the MECs, already in residence in a cell or in a group of cells?

We suggest this is accomplished by propagation of the recall stimuli, a process of chain reaction biofeedbacks and parallel processings through the neural networks and the lymphatic and vascular channels of the psychoneuroimmunology systems.

As an example, I think "right big toe," I think "raise toe up, then flex at the proximal joint."

Each of these acts is initiated by a sensory stimuli and leads to a motor response. In this case, I'm searching for the paths these thoughts take.

The motive for this witch hunt is to find the head waters for thoughts which become the rivers of ideas or the MECs that cut the channels that direct the course of the stream of our decisions, actions and creations.

MECs are restricted to the languages and stimuli of our birthright. Without additional learning, MECs will be stored in one's native tongue.

Webster Dictionary defines thinking as; 1. "mental concentration of ideas as distinguished from sense perceptions or emotion; the arranging of ideas in the mind."

2. "Mental concentration on ideas without perceptions or emotions."

3. "Idea: a product of reflection or mental concentration."

It is hard to believe that ideas are devoid of emotions.

Whenever one says, "I think I'll go for a walk or a ride," it is the boredom of the moment or the anticipation of a future trip, etc., that "lights the lamp," as Admiral Rickover does to his students. This is a pure response to an Emotion.

"I'm sure that ideas come and go in the brain, swirling and bubbling like a pot of hot soup cooking on the stove, never being articulated. As the heat rises, will the bubbles burst into consciousness or subconsciousness? This is the birth of an idea, initiating the Propagations that recall the MECs.

Dr. Bruce Brown

July 23, 1993

Hugh S. Lusted
Biocontrol Systems
430 Cowper St.
Palo Alto, CA 94301

Dr. Hugh Lusted:

The article "Body English," *Scientific American*, August 1993, is a "giant leap for science." Here are a few ideas that may compliment the research you're doing.

I'm an 81-year-old retired doctor, who has been evolving a theory of brain function for 20-plus years for "Accelerated Rehabilitation of the Hemiplegic." Your article is very thought-provoking.

Your statement, "muscles and eyes are under or controlled by brain waves," is but the tip of the iceberg.

Please consider the concept that emotions are the stimuli that initiate brain waves for thoughts, decisions, actions and creations. Emotion may be conscious, sub-conscious, subliminal, but are always involuntary.

The word "emotion" is misleading but it has incredible all-controlling power over brain waves and all their ramifications.

Survival and reproduction are the original emotions that evolved from the primordial soup to <u>prevent extinction of any species</u>. All subsequent emotions stem from these two and can be catalogued as exciting or inhibiting for the metabolic equilibrium of any living organism.

Any emotion's effectiveness will be proportional to its derived linkage to the original two.

The pervasiveness of emotions in creating brain waves is the core of this theory of brain function.

THE MECHANICS OF PRODUCING BRAIN WAVES BY EMOTIONS AND BODY CELL RESPONSES TO EMOTIONS

All cells have evolved receptors to receive stimuli. Stimuli are catalyzed by the receptors into MECs, a new terminology for cell memory.

MECs are recalled when new stimuli are received, catalyzed and stored as New MECs. This is the Learning Process.

Recall is the chain reaction biofeedback and parallel processing by neural networks and is the first of three steps of learning.

It is postulated that the stimuli of cell receptors and the receptors themselves are neuropeptides. There is some evidence that DNA and RNA are neuropeptides.

I presume that you would not be adverse to some research that should be a great money-maker as well as a benefit to hemiplegics. Joseph Kennedy was crippled with a stroke and would have willingly paid a fortune for a rapid restoration of his faculties. Your research should have tremendous application for "Accelerated Rehabilitation of the Hemiplegic."

I am enclosing a copy of the above paper which I will be happy for you to use any way you see fit. This is free of charge, if you can use it. I will be pleased if you can work out a plan to help the hemiplegic. This letter is your authority.

Dr. Bruce Brown

April 17, 1990

Dr. Norman Cousins
UCLA School of Medicine   REV; 12-17-95
Department of Psychoneuroimmunology

Dear Dr. Cousins:

Your book "Head First" has "lit my lamp" or "turned my crank" as my step-grandson says. I am impressed with your ideas about emotions.

Emotions are the centerpiece of my 20 years of trying to evolve a theory of brain function and a plan to accelerate the rehabilitation of the hemiplegic.

Your objective is to provide a healing process by demonstrating how positive and optimistic emotions can improve their condition. My objective is to return the hemiplegic some measure of self-control with emotions.

First premise is that brain and body cells share the ability to respond to stimuli and, second; that emotions catalyze stimuli into responses. For example: love, laughter, fear, hunger, hate, etc., are emotions that stimulate the symphony of responses through the vascular, neural and lymphatic channels of the Psychoneuroimmunology Systems to every cell of the body.

The theory conjectures that emotions have molecular and atomic configurations with electromotive forces (EMFs) and polarities (PS). They catalyze the electromotive forces (EMFs) and the polarities (PS) of intra- and extra-cellular stimuli into motor responses. Stimuli intensities, repetitions, durations and timings will have a direct bearing on the (EMFs) and (PS) of the responses.

The reception and/or perception of stimuli will be catalyzed into "exciting or inhibiting" responses, which will insure or enhance "survival and reproduction. Achieving homeostasis will help to prevent extinction of the species.

The responses required for rehabilitation of the hemiplegic, as well as performing everyday acts, will depend on emotions being stimulated with electromotive forces (EMFs) and polarities (PS) to elicit desired responses. This stimulation is cognitive, conscious but non-volitional.

I humbly submit that the amazing results of the melanoma study described on page 264 of "Head First" are involuntary responses and would have been impossible to achieve by the patients alone without you, Dr. Fawzy, et al, "lighting the lamps." We have neither "will power or won't power," but are slaves to our emotions.

"No matter what reason tells a man,
It is only when his emotions are
Are appealed to and enlisted
That he speaks from his heart."

Neurotransmitters, antibodies, enzymes, endocrines, endorphins, enkephalins, interferons, neuropeptides, etc., are but some of the stimuli interacting with cell receptors to catalyze responses. Receptors and their responses are Memory-Emotion-Concepts (MECs) capable of catalyzing (New-MECs) responses, in chain reaction propagations.

In tracing the origin of MECs, it is postulated that emotions evolved with the beginning of life to insure survival and reproduction of the species.

Such emotions are the memories and education (engrams), evolved over eons of time, which account for our thoughts, decisions, actions and creations of today. These are our inherited conditioned reflexes.

When the neuropeptides of recall are catalyzed by the MECs in any cell responses initiate Propagations. This is the process of chain reaction biofeedbacks, and parallel processings through the neural networks, and through the vascular and lymphatic channels of the Psychoneuroimmunology systems that link every cell of the body with every other cell. This will recall all the facets of information and programming contained in the recalled MECs.

Decisions arise from the foundations of our hereditary instincts of survival and reproduction but are molded and shaped by the environmental influences and pressures we sustain from the moment of fertilization of the ovum and throughout life.

In the primordial soup we started as one-celled organisms and today we have 100 billion neurons, 100 trillion connections between axons and dendrites and trillions of body cells all communicating with our neurons.

The significance of any MECs will be proportional to the percentages and intensities of their components of punishment and reward.

MECs are non-volitional emotions, and contrary to common beliefs, not governed by reason and logic.

The principles are the same as we ascend the evolutionary ladder.

The key theme is that Memories, alias Engrams of Education, alias MECs, alias Conditioning, are essential to receive and perceive the stimuli to which the brain and body are subjected. Stimuli may originate from two sources;

A. INTERNAL; The permanent programmed memories in the DNA, which control the autonomic functions of physiology, catalyzing the stimuli from physiologic changes in the body into motor responses which then act as stimuli to return the body to a state of equilibrium.

B. EXTERNAL; The continuously modified programmed memories in the body cells catalyze sensory stimuli into motor responses by chain reaction biofeedbacks and parallel processings. They are stored as New MECs and increase the sum of one's learning.

The stimuli from A. and B. propagate, discriminate and summate the thoughts, decisions, actions and creations.

Dr. Bruce Brown

The programmed instructions of the DNA and the RNA are MECs, catalyzing the neuropeptide stimuli they receive and perceive into motor responses. These responses create the succession of neuropeptides that trigger the growth processes of the fertilized ovum, initiating the schedules for the maturation of the newborn, the growth of a tree, and for all living processes.

My theories for rehabilitation are predicted on the capricious destruction of brain organization, which leaves myriad areas of normal but inaccessible hardware.

Brain and body cell functions, reduced to a one-cell operation, postulate that all body cells function as receptors.

When "neuropeptide" stimuli are catalyzed by the receptors in the cells the responses create MECs, which are engrams of knowledge, fathering our thoughts, ideas, decisions, actions and creations.

The telephone switchboard is a well-known example of a catalyst. The programmed relays of the switchboard are the emotion concept engrams and memories in our cells. When a number is dialed, the stimulus impulse will ring the receiving phone.

When a MECs is stimulated the response will depend on the molecular configurations of the stimulus and the concept.

Immune reactions to antigens (allergies) are familiar catalytic phenomenons. The sudden withdrawal of the hand touching a hot stove is a catalytic response to the emotion pain. The emotions of immunity and pain are catalysts leading to the responses but not a part of them, awaiting the next stimuli.

An infinite number of stimuli-catalysis-response events are required in a lifetime to create our stores of MECs of education and memories.

We are all familiar with the 1,000-plus falls to perfect the walking ability of the toddler. We all know the hours of practice to hone the coordination skills of the pianist or tennis player.

Following is a schematic portrayal of the responses elicited by our emotions as an example of how our brain and body cells function:

There are many facets to the psychoneuroimmunology healing process:

1. Restoring homeostasis is the purpose of the healing process. This is, first, a genetic survival trait.

2. Acquired conditioned reflexes may enhance and augment the healing process.

3. Involving genetic and acquired reflexes will depend on the stimuli intensities, duration, timing and repetition and may be cognitive, conscious or subconscious but are not volitional.

4. Stimuli may be external and assail our sensory systems or may be internal reflex response stimuli from our genetic or conditioned MECs, the feedback principle. They, too, are not volitional.

5. Consequently, stimuli from the counselor, minister, physician, family, friend, etc., or from some major event in the life of the patient will be only as effective as the degree they may impinge on the emotional profile of that person. The patient cannot consciously initiate a stimulus.

6. There are many adjunctive stimuli that enhance the healing process, beyond a person's control, such as laughter, love, commitment to and involvement in something other than their own little world. Even fear, worry, anger, jealously, greed, pride, vanity, conceit, ambition, etc., may be helpful in forcing or shocking one out of a complacency of Hemostasis or a quagmire of self-pity, apathy, despair or surrender.

Applying psychoneuroimmunology to the rehabilitation of the hemiplegic:

The intense emotional trauma of the hemiplegic is well-known. Just as a dire diagnosis of cancer can cripple the patient's will to fight, so the crippled state of hemiplegia severs all neural pathways between brain and body. The lifetime development of neural pathway communication tracts for physical and many mental skills, have been totally destroyed. There are no known medical or surgical remedies.

No amount of coaxing, scolding, rewarding or punishing can alter the life sentence of solitary confinement and imprisonment within his own body.

Can skin-applied muscle stimulators become reflex conditioners when activated simultaneously with multiple MECs stimuli?

Is there communication from the brain and/or body cells through the blood stream or intact nerve tracts by neuropeptides, endocrines, hormones, etc.?

Stimuli can communicate with the sensory systems.

It is hoped that when the hemiplegic sees and feels his muscles respond to the stimuli the EMFs and PS of the feed-back stimuli will be so intense as to create new pathways, new memories and new engrams of education that are volitional.

Dr. Cousins:

Religion is a powerful emotion of the human animal yet you make no mention of it. Any reason?

My views are that religion was created by mankind to protect him from and ward off all the unseen and unknown powers of the universe.

Thanking you for a very thought-provoking book, I am
Sincerely BB.

Dr. Bruce Brown

METAPHYSICS

EVOLUTION OF RELIGION

"THERE ARE NO ATHEISTS IN FOX HOLES."

Religion is one of the most dominant of all emotion concepts for insuring survival and reproduction of a species. The concept has its origin in the beginning of life.

When single-cell organisms were first created in the primordial ooze, their survival and reproduction were based on their ability to distinguish environmental supportive conditions from those destructive.

This is the "Yes" and "No"; the "Plus" and "Minus"; or the "Right" and "Wrong".

Ascending the evolutionary ladder, survival was enhanced by the "herd and flock instincts and gregariousness," which provided greater security and protection.

Grouping into colonies offered new genetic material for reproduction and specie diversification.

Group harmony led to concepts of, "What's For Me" and "What's For You." The first for the individual's survival and the second for reproduction and parenting.

When people banded together for common good, divisions of labor sprung up, special skills developed, benefiting everyone. Differences of opinion and pecking orders evolved. Ethical and moral codes were formulated, with a loss of some individual independence but a gain in security and the mutual assistance of sharing.

Always there were the unseen forces such as the Ice Age, earthquakes, tornadoes, volcanic eruptions, floods, famine, droughts, plagues, death, accidents, lightning, cancer, sickness, birth defects, strokes, etc.

The "Fears of These Unknowns" created ideologies, superstitions, tribal rituals, sacrifices, religious charms and trappings, incantations to ward off evil spirits. Greek and Roman mythology dictated rules for community and personal conduct. As time went on, this was superseded by deities such as Zoroaster, Buddha, Mohammed, Confucius and the Christian God.

The Bible, Torah and Koran prescribed the laws and teachings of those religions. Holy wars and crusades slaughtered "infidels" in the name of religion.

Cultural differences led to a great diversity of religions. Worship often was and is self-indulgence of past sins or follies and advance payment for future indiscretions. Even the taking of pills and going to a doctor are based on hopes and beliefs that the evil spirits of sickness will go away.

No matter how many problems science solves and man's longevity is extended, mankind's mortality is inevitable. We evolve our own codes of ethical and moral conduct, to go by volition and will-power are responses to our MECs as received and/or perceived in our lives.

Our codes of conduct may be conscious or subconscious but always non-volitional. This is a serious blow to one's ego, but humility is a very becoming grace.

Hebrews 11:1:

"Faith is the substance of things hoped for, the evidence of things not seen."

Thomas Jefferson, June 21, 1807:

"His (the medical student) mind must be strong, if, arising above juvenile credulity, it can maintain a wise infidelity against the authority of his instructors, and the bewitching delusions of their theories." GRAMPS

Dr. Fesmire and Rev. Waldrop:

Thought you might be interested that the hymn "Open My Eyes" was the inspiration 20 years ago to formulate a theory of brain and body cell functions. The two functions are inseparable. The goal was to discover or devise a way to "Accelerate the Rehabilitation of the Hemiplegic," who lives in a kind of hell.

"Open my eyes; place in my hands; open my ears; and open my mouth," refer to sensory organs of sight, touch, hearing; with speech as a corollary. "Open my heart" reveals the true person — the soul, if you wish — residing in our emotions. Sensory organs are the doors through which environmental stimuli of learning blend with the resident hereditary knowledge.

Dr. Bruce Brown

"To forgive" implies a complete abdication of one's selfishness, vanity, conceit, pride and greed.

It does not imply an absence of the instincts of survival and reproduction, without which we would cease to exist.

Undoubtedly it is God's plan for harmonizing all living creatures be they animal, plant, fungi, protists and moneras (including bacteria and blue-green algae) which divides the world's 10 million known species into five kingdoms.

True forgiveness is a status God asks us to achieve, and yet recognizes our frailties along the path.

This is one man's code of ethics, seeking understanding, but not necessarily agreement.

Eternity

"To see the world in a grain of sand is to hold all eternity in the palm of your hand." author Unknown

To see life in a single cell in each of the five kingdoms of our world, e.g. animals, plants, fungi, protists and monera, takes the wisdom of a Solomon.

Life in the five kingdoms took millions of years to unfold.

All life is predicated on Survival and Reproduction.

All life had a beginning with stimuli, followed by responses.

In mankind, responses lead to thinking, then decisions, followed by actions and producing creations, original for each individual.

Thoughts in the infant stages are dependent on the parents or their caretakers. Directing the course of a child's thoughts is a sacred mission.

Thoughts will be the reflection of one's knowledge.

For learning and knowledge to grow, one must be able to recall, modify and restore them.

The intensity of learning and knowledge will be directly proportional to the emotional content of the stimuli.

All knowledge is stored as Memory-Emotion-Concepts or MECs as a convenient way of understanding thinking.

Mountains and valleys, tops and bottoms, highs and lows, hot and cold, wet and dry, smooth and rough, well and sick, happy and sad, pep and fatigue, fat and thin, beginnings and ends are some of the dimensions of our world. There are many gradations between one extreme and the other.

These are but a few of the wonders of GOD, the supreme creator of our world and all the wonders of outer space. We have arrived at the "Big Bang" as the best explanation of the origin of our world.

"Beginnings: are all that we have at this point in understanding what created mankind and what God disposes.

Beginnings of life would be single cells, followed by groups of cells endowed with the gifts of life, and the prerequisites for survival and reproduction.

Beginnings occurred in the primordial ooze, where trials and errors created the neuropeptides and the MECs as the tools for learning and memory.

Recalled MECs provoke thoughts, decisions, actions and creations. These were then modified into New MECs, inducing the scope of expanding learning.

Some of the gifts of life were immortalized in the hymn, "Open My Eyes That I May See."

This hymn illuminates the "Spirit Divine" wherein sensory stimuli produce motor responses.

This transcends all forms of life whether mankind, animal, bird, vegetable or microscopic organisms.

When God created lives of all kinds he endowed all of them with two basic requirements, e.g. instincts for Survival and Reproduction.

All forms of life fulfill these requirements according to the master plans of our Creator. Failure leads to extinction. Each form has its "disaster plans" for healing, escaping and adapting to environmental challenges, finding a mate for propagation or evolving parthenogenesis.

EXAMPLES OF STIMULI TO RESPONSES IN ALL LIVING FORMS

In all animals a tissue wound immediately begins to heal. Anger, attack or flight take place under stress. Sweating and insulin production are in response to changes in the body chemistry. Removing an early cancer may save a life.

In the plant world, sawing off a tree branch immediately stimulates bark production to cover the wound. Planting the vegetable garden will fail without supplying the plant's needs for fertilizer, water, sun and viable temperatures.

Germs can kill unless the proper treatments are started early. We often fail to appreciate the defensive actions the body takes to preserve our well-being.

LETTER TO THE GRANDCHILDREN OF MY BEST FRIEND, ROY PARKER, AND IN HONOR OF THE "SOCRATES" OF PADUCAH, JOHN T. SCOPES

After 84 years of living, there are some thoughts and philosophies a grandfather might pass on. As a close friend of Grandpa Parker, this is what he wanted me to tell you.

Throughout life you will be facing decisions at every turn. To solve any problems that confront you, defining them is one-half of their solution.

The other half is where grandpaw's advice comes in handy. Understanding how you think and how your emotions control thoughts, decisions, actions and creations will help you to see all sides of any problems and make informed responses.

From the moment the fertilized egg starts to grow in your mother's womb you will become the sum of all the responses to the stimuli of the emotions you inherited from the primordial ooze, where evolution first began, plus those acquired since birth.

You will have neither "will power or won't power," but will respond according to the intensity, repetition, timing and duration of the stimulation from your emotions.

These stimuli may be hereditary or environmental in origin. Your responses to these emotion stimuli will be stored as MECs. This will create and store all of the knowledge you will ever possess.

The secret of brain and cell function lies in the ability of MECs to be recalled, modified and restored as a new MECs. This is how we add to our knowledge.

The source, course and goal of the universe is unknown and beyond human understanding, possibly and probably forever. Many things will be difficult to understand. Why one person is born to grace and success and another to misery and failure will be difficult to explain.

Death, war, plagues, drought, floods, catastrophes of nature and pestilence strike without warning and without rhyme or reason. Different religions evolved in the human races of the world to try and explain these mysteries.

Change what you can and accept the rest.

Be tolerant and humble. The more you know, the more you will appreciate how much you don't know. Have pride but use it wisely. "Think without confusion clearly and act from honest motives purely." Whatever you choose to do in life, do it with distinction and honor.

Lou Holtz, Notre Dame coach: "Ability is what you're capable of doing. Motivation determines what you do. Attitude determines how well you do it."

This letter and the enclosed article are the distilled essence of my philosophies. They are contributions to your character development and to a happy and successful life.

Affectionately, your grandfather's friend
Bruce Brown, MD

PS: Read this once a year until 20 years old. "Your Gramp's wishes"??

"TELL ME ABOUT YOUR GOD", SERMON 8/25/95 (FESMIRE)

As a small child the parent, usually the father, is the omnipotent one in our life, love predominates, permissiveness and encouragement are freely dispensed, and security is home.

Then freedom and adventure expand the parameters of knowledge and activity, with complete faith that security, help and understanding will always be available at home.

"As the twig is bent so inclineth the tree," Alexander Pope.

This paraphrases as; If parents believe in and encourage religious participation early in life, the child will acquire an acceptance and respect for God.

If we are deep-down honest with ourselves, it will be obvious that we need a belief in God as the answer for the thousands of miracles and mysteries that encompass us throughout life.

"There are no atheists in a foxhole, in wartime."

So, Wayne, you see I did listen to your sermon and enjoyed your question.

Dr. Bruce Brown

OTHER TOPICS

SUICIDE

The ultimate in resolve is the question of whether an individual has the "will or won't power" to seek assistance to die for pain and suffering for an intractable and terminal health condition. Emotions control and direct thinking, deciding, acting and creating. Therefore, the decision to seek assistance to die is controlled by the patients' emotions. No one has the right to do more than offer advice and assistance.

This refers to the furor over Dr. Kevorkian's assisting a person in a dignified and painless relief from inescapable death.

Does the individual have certain "unalienable rights of life, liberty and the pursuit of happiness?" — Declaration of Independence.

To plead the case for the terminally ill patient, consider the role emotions play as, one by one, the independence of self-control, hoping to see their children find careers, assuring a spouse's future welfare, as the storm clouds of impending death, draw steadily nearer. Jackie Onassis died after a relatively rapid cancer growth. She requested no further treatment and a return to her home. She exercised her right to die as she had been taught.

From all accounts, Dr. Kevorkian feels he is not taking a life but assisting a patient to the Nirvana of the next world.

Survival is the instinct emotion of an individual and reproduction is the instinct emotion of sharing, parenting and inter-dependence between peoples.

Emotions may be conscious, subconscious and subliminal but they are always involuntary.

In conclusion, the request for help to escape the pain and total despair of a trip to death is an emotional right of the individual. That decision is a summation of all the hereditary and acquired stimuli received from the moment of conception 'til time of death. It is an involuntary decision.

My 45-year-old daughter is dying of spreading brain cancer for the past 15 months. She is fully aware of her condition and its relentless downhill course. Not long ago she questioned me, "Dad, how long must I wait for the pain to go away?"

For young children the father is the omnipotent source of all wisdom and comfort in times of stress. In the agony of her condition she came to her father, whose feet of clay failed her in her final days of agony. Jesus called to "Abba" when faced with crucifixion, but received no answer.

Assisted death can be one of the most merciful acts one human being could give another. Instead of taking a life you may be giving eternal life! We don't need to think twice about putting a crippled or sick animal to death.

The two most powerful and basic emotions for all living organisms are survival and reproduction. Extinction of a species results without them. All of the millions of emotions to which mankind is heir are merely derivatives of these two. The potency of any emotion is directly proportional to the percentages of these two basic instinctual requirements. Emotions control our desire and rights for an assisted dying.

UNKNOWNS

The source, course and goal of the Universe is unknown and beyond human understanding, possibly and probably forever.

The unknown may be for good or bad; right or wrong; fearful or hopeful; holy or unholy. Lack of understanding may be an enhancement or threat to survival and reproduction.

Consequently we have "projected, extended or expanded (known date or experience) into an area not known or experienced so as to arrive at a usual conjectural knowledge of the unknown area."

This extrapolates into God, "the Supreme and Ultimate Reality" who created the universe.

Further exploration lead to natural science or physics, defined as: "a science that deals with matter and energy and their interactions in the fields of mechanics, acoustics, optics, heat, electricity, magnetism, radiation, atomic structure and nuclear phenomenon."

The interaction of matter and energy (known data or experience) conjectures into electromotive forces, polarities or valences. This extrapolates into the conjecture that stimulus energy will lead to response energy, which is the basis for the theory of brain function presented.

This conjectures that stimuli from the (External) environment and/or the (Internal) heredity interact with the atoms and molecules of cells to formulate or program MECs. The atomic molecular chain configurations of MECs are the engrams of education (Memories). These MECs are the programs found in every cell. A MECs at any point in time of our lives will reflect all of the stimuli received throughout life up to that moment. MECs propagate, discriminate and summate the received and/or perceived stimuli into ever changing programs and their responses.

The programs are directly related to stimuli intensities, durations, timings and repetitions. Comparable to the population vectors described by the John Hopkin's Georgopoulos team.

2. SUBCONSCIOUSNESS, "thought, feeling and behavior without awareness."

It is said that we begin to die the moment of birth. The major realm of brain function is subconsciousness.

Hunger, thirst, cold, love, hate, etc., begin long before we are aware of them.

Our metabolic equilibrium proceeds apace whether we are asleep or awake. It is only when we become aware of stimuli reception and perception that we have consciousness.

The interaction of stimuli being catalyzed into responses by the MECs is completely involuntary.

UNKNOWNS CREATE OUR MECs REGARDLESS OF AGE

1. The INFANT; The parameter stimuli of an infant or newborn animal are the parents and/or siblings, his immediate environment, and his instincts, such as hunger, thirst, need of parental protection, training and loving care. All of these are Unknowns and beyond his control.

Some of the exciting MECs that will be programmed are security, faith, trust and contentment, etc.; the inhibiting MECs will be fear, pain, discomfort, misery, etc. They will either enhance his metabolic equilibrium or threaten it. This early programming of his MECs will be the foundation stones of his personality and behavior, illustrating how parents can play a major role.

2. The ADULT; The parameter stimuli of the growing adult will be the parents, teachers, friends and peers. These are Unknowns until

the MECs evaluate the stimuli as he or she receives or perceives them. His environment will expose him to the Unknowns of illness, cancer, accidents, catastrophes of natures, poverty, ostracism, etc. If these stimuli are Exciting he will be secure, successful, humble, sharing and happy.

If they are Inhibiting he may become obnoxious, selfish, greedy, vain, bigoted, afraid and lonely.

The underlying principles of continuation of the species are Survival and Reproduction.

Fear of the Unknowns are the basis of our superstitions and the ancient worship of gods, rituals to ward off the evil spirits, rituals to appease the gods of famine, drought, pestilence and defeat by the enemy.

The shamans, oracles and prophets arose to counter the fears. The present-day doctors and the taking of pills is an outgrowth of this.

All the Religions, including mythology, arose to insure our survival and reproduction. Hope and Faith are the epitome of man's helplessness in a world beyond comprehension and understanding of the Unknowns. Love and Caring evolved for reproduction and protection through our herd instincts and colonies. Man is not an island alone.

COMPANION PAPER TO "UNKNOWNS", SO MY GRANDCHILDREN WILL NOT THINK GRAMPS IS AN ATHEIST OR AGNOSTIC

I firmly believe in and financially contribute to the churches to which I have belonged. Churches are a potent force in our lives as a code of ethics that differentiate us from the small child whose principle aim in life is to receive, whether it is love, food, security, comfort, entertainment, play or attention.

All religions, of which there are many, are based on the sharing between people as opposed to individualism. Essentially it insures survival and reproduction. The rewards of society must be greater than egocentrism, or love and friendship would never have evolved.

I cannot believe prayer does anything more than to give comfort to the one who prays. The laws of nature created us, bestowed many gifts upon us, and has arranged a time for us to return to atoms and molecules until such time as God devises some more advanced programs.

Our current set of nature's laws decree that we carry out the programs that we inherit, live in peace and harmony with our fellow man, pass the baton to our children, and leave the world a little better off for our contributions here on earth.

There is nothing to be gained by worrying.

"Four things a man must do,
　if he would make his record true,
To think without confusion clearly,
To act from honest motives purely,
To trust in heaven and God securely and
To love your fellow man sincerely."
Van Dyke

"So live that when thy summons comes, thou go, not like a quarry slave scourged to his dungeon, but like one who wraps the draperies of his couch about him and lies down to pleasant dreams."　Thanatopsis

Gramps

ANATOMY OF THE EMOTION CONCEPT MEC CANCER

PROPAGATIONS, DISCRIMINATIONS AND SUMMATIONS OF FEAR, TERROR, DEATH, ETC.

There are few MECs more threatening to survival than cancer. Reproduction, the other requirement for preservation and continuation of a species, is a negligible factor.

The predictable unpredictability of Cancer raises the specter of the Unknowns, those stimuli that inspire the MECs of Fear, Terror, Death, etc., creating nightmares that haunt and motivate our lives. It isn't only receiving the stimuli, but the perception of those stimuli that paralyzes the victim. Each individual has his own set of interpretations, which can be devastating for some.

Each of us have evolved our own set of values for the life we lead. None of us are sure what awaits us in the hereafter. Unshakable conviction that God has a place for us is a comforting thought. On the other hand, being torn away from our families and home, with many hopes, aspirations and ambitions unfinished, is difficult to reconcile. And yet we all know that death is inevitable.

Perhaps the "Thanatopsis" expressed it best in "like one who wraps the draperies of the couch about him and lies down to pleasant dreams."

Looking back on 84 years, many imperfections and a few perfections, I feel that I summated my acquired and inherited emotion concepts into memories, thoughts, decisions, actions and creations as responses to the stimuli I received and perceived. This is the way God ordained it and it is a judgment I must accept and try to lie down to pleasant dreams.

I am now 84 years of age and it has been a long three months since my wife died on my birthday, May 26, 1992. I am eating, sleeping and working with little enthusiasm. I have a puppy for company, a woman to clean once a week and a daughter within 1/2 mile who calls and comes frequently. I'm trying to maintain the gardens my wife so dearly loved but there is very little purpose to it all. I should like to remarry but am afraid it would be very unfair to anyone trying to replace 50 years of a very happy marriage.

At this point in time, I don't care much what happens to me. I have not found any dedication to any activity to help.

My greatest pleasure and ambition is to perfect my ideas on brain function which have met with "No" reception at every turn. Each of us in life "marches to a different drummer" and the researchers have their own projects and ideas and have no room for a renegade philosophy, even though I'm convinced I've made a major breakthrough.

RANDOM THOUGHTS

This was paraphrased in 340 BC by Plato; "Ask a man the right question and he will find the truth for himself."

NEURAL NETWORKS

Reactions to severe shocks to one's MECs, such as fear, shame, grief, hate, etc., can overwhelm cognition, consciousness and subconsciousness and block chain-reaction biofeedbacks, parallel processings and the neural networks. This may lead to withdrawal from reality, avoidance of painful situations, inability to block or erase painful memories or determination to seek revenge. Depressions, psychosis, manic states, hysteria and even suicide or murder may result.

1. The teenager's hormones (pheromone-neuropeptides) appear in puberty and the reproductive impulses appear with a sudden interest in and a response from the opposite sex.

2. Profuse sweating after a day of hard work in the summer sun, produces neuropeptides resulting from electrolyte depletion and stimulating the demand for fluid replacement.

3. Neuropeptides recall the evolutionary demands of nature. The MECs of reproduction initiate a string of responses. The butterfly egg hatches into a caterpillar. The caterpillar eats leaves, spins a cocoon around itself, and emerges as a new butterfly.

4. Angry bees sting the nearest person who disturbs their hive and fire ants sting the first bare skin. Survival neuropeptides are catalyzed by the hereditary MECs programs of the bees and ants. The victim's neuropeptides created by the pain of the stings are catalyzed into the instant retaliation of killing the insects or beating a hasty retreat.

HOW NEURAL NETWORKS INITIATE OUR LEARNING PROCESSES

The easiest way to explain is to take a commonplace scene of life and try to interpret it. "The first hour of each day." When the alarm goes off; we're slept out; or a haunting worry from the previous day prods us; we check the clock and review the upcoming demands of the day. Whatever the reason, we begin a recall of the hidden emotions that drive us all, subconsciously or involuntarily even though our ego denies it. We may automatically use the bathroom, get dressed, and sally forth for that "cup of coffee" that many people need to rejoin the human race and reestablish continuity of their life.

Neural networking initiates consciously, subconsciously and involuntarily the first step of brain function, which is propagation of our recalled MECs. The flow of thoughts begins with "what to wear," or a review of the wardrobe; the anticipated response we wish to elicit for ourselves first and foremost and then for the reactions from others. The decision and selection can only transpire by recalling the MECs which reside in each and every cell.

Step 1. The process of chain reaction biofeedbacks, where each MECs will recall closely - related MECs through all the stored memories until the recalls are too distant and weak to remember;

Step 2. Parallel processings or the simultaneous orders from he brain, such as "pull out the drawers, open the closet, and try on the clothes" to assist the decision making.

Step 3. Call on "neural networks," the complex nerve fibers interconnecting all the cells involved, to provide impetus to start feedbacks and parallel processings. Neural networking starts your car's engine, turns on dashboard lights and offers the various options of shifting gears, accelerating to different speeds, braking, turning, observing speed limits, avoiding pedestrians, etc.

LEARNING BY EXPERIENCE

Biofeedback chain reactions and parallel processings via neural networks are the means of creating more MECs, which become the bank of knowledge. The range of learning is almost infinite. There are 50 billion brain neurons all inter-connected through the axons and dendrites. Learning to walk or to throw a baseball requires thousands of repetitions to perfect one's skills. Each act of repetition recalls the learned knowledge (Old MECs) resulting from prior trials and errors. Each improvement in performance adds the rewards of satisfaction and each error adds the punishment of failure. Rewards or punishments of repetition create New MECs. As long as "practice makes perfect" learning will continue and, if failure becomes too punishing, learning will stop.

HABITS

SMOKING, OBESITY, ALCOHOLISM, HABITS AND DRUGS 1987-1993; REVISED 10/8/93

If our theory of brain and nerve functions is right, addictions and habits result when noxious or innocuous stimuli are received or perceived by cells and catalyzed into MECs. The stimuli will have intensity, duration, timing and repetition, creating the conditioned learning and programming of that cell, whether harmful or innocuous. It is conjectured that stimuli are neuropeptides.

DEFINITION OF HABITS: "An acquired or developed mode of behavior or function that has become nearly or completely involuntary."

Learning habits is no different in principle than a small child learning the spelling of his name plus the shapes of the alphabetical letters. The stimuli are supplied by the teachers, the parents, siblings, etc., plus the hereditary drive to emulate and please the instructors. Learning from teachers and carrying out one's internal programming is an evolutionary requirement of survival. It is an Inborn Subconscious Drive. It earns the praise rewards from the teachers and it drives a newborn foal to search for the rewarding milk in the nipples.

The addictions of smoking, over-eating, alcoholism and becoming prey to drugs follows the same learning patterns as the learning and establishment of habits.

The smoking addiction usually results from the desire to be one of the gang or to emulate someone we admire. Once started it becomes a safety valve to release internal anxieties.

The gluttony addiction may be a trait of the entire family; a consolation when rejected by peers; an escape from boredom; a craving to fill the over-distended stomach; or an action to prove one's independence, defying usual customs, or drawing attention to bolster the ego.

Alcohol addiction, beyond the occasion drink, is a self-rewarding escape and an announcement to the world that "I am dependent on no one and in complete control of myself," in other words, an ego trip.

Drug addiction is an escape into Nirvana, often starting as an experiment, but soon resulting in a craving beyond self-control. Intravenous anesthetic drugs are beyond self-control but leave no residual craving.

As the learning of addictions and habits progresses they begin to dictate the victims actions through unremitting, Craving to Smoke, Insatiable Eating, Exhilaration of Alcohol, Comfort of a Longstanding Habit and a Torture-Driven Escape into the Nirvana of Drugs.

Cell functions are not isolated and solitary entities but interconnected through the blood stream, lymphatics, sensory systems, endocrines, etc., with the neural networks providing the chain reaction biofeedbacks and parallel processings between the MECs which are the units of knowledge and the programming in each cell. This is the basis of the science of Psychoneuroimmunology.

Consequently, replacing or modifying addicting MECs with New MECs, we must utilize all the intracellular connections, described above, in a a learning process. This will require the wisdom of a Solomon.

Learning is acquired by hard work and repetition, not by osmosis. Experience is a process of trial and error. Motivation is a hereditary God-given drive to succeed, plus inspiration and encouragement from parents, friends and strangers, as well as, the stimuli encountered from one's environment from the moment of conception throughout life.

Rewards and punishments will provide the incentive to modify or replace addictions. In summary; All of us receive, perceive or depend on involuntary stimuli to acquire our knowledge, make decisions, carry out actions, and construct creations uniquely our own. This process is totally dependent on outside stimuli, which is one of the most positive effects of all religions.

Christians get their support by sitting on the right hand of God the father; the Muslim from Islam and Allah; Buddhist from Buddha; Zoroastrians from Mazda; Confucians from Confucius; Early Greeks from the gods of mythology; African and American Indians from Shamanism, all of whom supply the impetus for learning. Defining a problem is often tantamount to solving that problem.

SUMMATION

Any memory-thought, decision, action or creation at any point in life is a summation of the EMFs and polarities of all our inner emotion concepts. These concepts are the distilled essence of our hereditary instincts and our acquired conditioning experiences.

Every word we choose and speak; every twitch of a muscle fiber; every body posture we assume; every physiological, psychological and neurological process will be a reflection of this summation.

The infinite complexity of the permutations and combinations of the 600,000 atoms in each neuron so arranged as to code our emotions in molecular configurations is staggering. Then add 10,000 dendrites for each neuron to receive stimuli and catalyze these into motor responses to 200 billion other neurons and you will still only be considering the central nervous system.

Manipulation of emotion concepts in the human race whether for good or evil might, at first glance, sound like Frankenstein. In reality, we are doing just that in our daily contacts with others. The way we dress; the words we speak; the acts we perform are all directed to manipulate another person. The entire range of advertising; the advice from the doctor; the rules and laws of society to do the same.

The purpose of this book is not to change people but to help them understand how the brain works. We shall always have Survival and Reproduction with us. There will always be "What's for Me" and What's for You." Hopefully, better understanding of ourselves will lead to a happier life and we will minimize our injury to others.

NOTES

NOTES

NOTES

Printed in the USA
CPSIA information can be obtained
at www.ICGtesting.com
JSHW080003150824
68134JS00021B/2249

9 781681 623368